The Modern History Manual

Study Skills for History at A level and beyond.

J.A. Cloake, V. Crinnion, S.M. Harrison.

The Authors:

J.A. Cloake was educated at Durham, Cambridge and Manchester Universities. He is currently Head of History at Knutsford County High School, Cheshire, and is an examiner in O level History and A level Politics and Government.

V. Crinnion was educated at Swansea and Calgary Universities. He is currently Head of Humanities at Leftwich High School, Northwich. Publications include: 'The Great Rebellion', 'Science and Superstition' and 'The Great War 1914-18' (1986) [Macmillan: History in Depth]. He has also contributed an essay on A level History to 'The History Curriculum' (ed. C Portal, 1986).

S.M. Harrison was educated at Lancaster University. He is currently Humanities Advisor for the London Borough of Havering. He has had eight years experience of A level examining. In 1981 the Royal Historical Society published his 'The Pilgrimage of Grace in the Lake Counties 1536-7', which won the Whitfield Prize. More recently he has written 'Elizabeth in Danger', 'Henry VIII and the Dissolution of the Monasteries', 'The Early Railways, 1825-1850' (1986) [Macmillan: History in Depth]. 'World Conflict in the Twentieth Century' [Macmillan: History in the Making].

Editors:

J.A. Cloake, Janet Day and Bren Abercrombie.

Acknowledgements:.

Thanks are due to our typists Miss G. Cloake and Mrs G. Childs, who have patiently and thoroughly transformed many ages of manuscript and to Mr M.E. Sykes who provided invaluable assistance at an early stage of this work. We are also indebted to our past and present Advanced level students at Knutsford County High School for the lessons which they have taught us and their help with this work. The publishers wish to thank Pamela Ebdon for assistance.

The authors are grateful to the Joint Matriculation Board and the London University Examination Board for permission to use quotations from their Examiners' Reports.

The writing of this book has been a co-operative effort, but co-ordination and editing was undertaken by J.A. Cloake, and illustrations, by V. Crinnion.

First published 1987 by

Framework Press Ltd
St Leonard's House
St Leonardgate
Lancaster LA1 1NN

The Modern History Manual

ISBN 1 85008 090 9

Illustrations by V. Crinnion

Cover design by John Angus

Typeset by Blackpool Typesetting Services Ltd, Blackpool

Printed and bound in Great Britain by
Redwood Burn Limited, Trowbridge, Wiltshire

Reprinted December 1987

For our parents

CONTENTS

'Free yourself from distractions . . .'

'. . . and make sure that you
have the right conditions
in which to work.'

INTRODUCTION

How you study can be as important as what you study. This book explains and demonstrates a range of basic skills required by History students. The enthusiasm shown by students and teachers for 'The History Manual' (Framework Press, 1985) has encouraged us to prepare this present work in which the same skills are set in the context of Modern English and European History. Through the practice of these skills, historical competence and understanding will be encouraged. Both in content and form this book attempts to take account of recent knowledge about how people learn and thus how their study methods may be improved.

It is important that students learn to develop effective and efficient methods of study within the context of specific subjects. All our experience as teachers confirms the view that students have extreme difficulty in applying over-generalised advice to particular subject matter or transferring study skills from a lesson to moments when they are left to organise themselves. For many new Advanced level students understanding of the subject and subsequent performance in examinations is seriously, perhaps permanently, undermined by inefficient and unthinking study methods. If students are poorly equipped to study and yet are faced with the greater demands of an Advanced level course, they cannot hope to make much progress. Consider, for instance, the finding that only 10% of classroom activity prior to the Sixth form involves reading; half of this is in short bursts of up to fifteen seconds. It cannot be surprising therefore that the work of many Advanced level students in this area is slow, dull and relatively unproductive.

Ultimately the study of Advanced level History should prepare students to be independent in their learning. Students should be able to generate interests and ideas, pursue them in a scholarly way and critically assess their findings.

What is in this book?

Each chapter concentrates on different skills. Various themes run through all the chapters;

active involvement and a critical attitude are two of the most dominant. In order to find out what each part of this book is about, read 'About this chapter' at the start of each section. The pattern adopted by each chapter is to give an explanation in the text and demonstrate with examples. In nearly all the chapters there are exercises. Students can try the majority of exercises unaided, but some are designed to be done with teacher guidance. The exercises are meant to develop an awareness of study in the student, whilst reinforcing knowledge of sixteenth century History.

How should you use this book?

When coming to this book for the first time, a student may use the skills of analytical reading, previewing and skimming through the book to get the feel of its layout and composition. Once the student has started the course, he or she should be able to read and work through the book carefully and progressively from 'Analytical Reading' to 'The Examination' during one term. Thereafter as work progresses, topics are covered or weaknesses reveal themselves, special attention may be given to the relevant sections of the book. Occasionally the teacher may direct students to a chapter which seems helpful. The teacher may choose to incorporate the practice of particular skills or aspects of historical study into lessons on certain topics during the course. Some parts of the book are concerned with the more difficult aspects of Advanced level History and may not be immediately accessible to a student at the start of the Sixth form course.

There are many assumptions about History in this book. Students may disagree with some of the points made. Such criticism is healthy and to be encouraged if it is based on experience and experiment which has changed their own methods for the better. What is to be discouraged is the belief that patterns of study cannot be improved and methods of working once fixed are unchallengeable. A more relevant dialogue between student and History, or between student and teacher, can only be valuable. It is hoped that this book will stimulate and contribute to that dialogue.

Is this your problem?

COPYING	RELEVANCE	INFORMATION
Not your own words!	*This is not to do with essay title!*	*There is not enough detail here.*
Page 38	Page 70, 94	Page 32, 42 ff.
NARRATIVE	BOOKS	LATE WORK
This is a 'story,' or an analysis.'	*Is this all you've read? check your list!*	*You are still one essay behind. Why?*
Page 14, 42, 77	Page 13, 27	Page 131
MAIN POINTS	ARRANGING IDEAS	EVIDENCE
You miss the main ideas — this is mere detail.	*This is muddled! Confused!*	*You don't try to support what you are arguing.*
Page 32, 42, 43	Page 77, 85, 87	Page 97
FACTS	STYLE	NOTES
Are you sure?? This is only your opinion.	*Clumsy. Not English! UNCLEAR! Inelegant.*	*Why are there so many gaps in your file?*
Page 113, 114	Page 100 ff.	Page 44, 128
LESSONS	BOOKS	LESSONS
Concentrate! Contribute more!	*This is an unsatisfactory source. Encyclopaedias?!*	*Ask questions when you don't understand*
Page 5, 44	Page 8, 14	Page 43, 44
NOTES	MEMORY	EXAMS
Which are your main headings? Copied up yet?	*You seem to have forgotten everything we did last....*	*Have you revised for this test?!*
Page 38, 39	Page 136	Page 124, 140

CHAPTER 1

ANALYTICAL READING

About this Chapter

A fundamental aspect of studying History in school and college is reading. A student can expect to spend the majority of his study-time involved in an activity that not only provides historical knowledge but also serves as a basis for other activities: writing essays, making notes and, of course, thinking about the subject. Too often, however, students read inefficiently and ineffectively. This chapter attempts to provide students with an elementary 'strategy' for reading which (a) does not make the usual assumptions about their competence and (b) provides a useful procedure by which history texts may be approached more analytically. It should provide a starting-point from which students can formulate their own, more individual strategies.

| EXERCISE | THE NEW EUROPE |

Read the extract below in your usual way:

The Industrial Revolution did more than free man from economic dependence on relatively static methods of production; it increased the total amount of food and goods available to every individual. Many people enjoyed a more ample and varied diet than ever before. For the first time a large number of laborers could afford to eat meat regularly. Sugar, citrus fruits, cocoa, were made available to a mass market. Tea and coffee, once luxury items, became standard drinks for every class. Shoes, clothing, furniture, toys, all were produced in increasing quantities at prices most people could afford. Industrial workers formed the chief market as well as the labor force of the new industrial society. On balance it can be said that the Industrial Revolution, with all its evils, brought a great increase in material prosperity to a majority of the members of the societies which it transformed. It is only necessary to compare the living conditions of laborers in nonindustrial areas with those of industrial workers, miserable as these may be in some cases, to be aware of the material benefits of the conversion to machine technology.

The revolution in the economy of Europe produced important changes in European society. Land, for centuries the economic base of the aristocracy, was no longer the chief source of wealth. New industries, finance capitalism, and commerce brought ever-increasing wealth to the middle classes. With mounting importunity these classes demanded political power to match their economic power, and through the greater part of the nineteenth century they challenged the political authority of the landed aristocracy. . . .

. . . The change in western Europe from a predominantly rural to a predominantly urban society had other important effects. A population concentrated in cities was more accessible to the influence of new ideological trends than a population scattered through the countryside. The man who had severed his traditional local ties to live in the impersonal and anonymous city searched for something he could identify with, for new loyalties and attachments. The city became the great center of the mass movements of the industrial age, the breeding ground of nationalist and socialist doctrines, of new religious sects, temperance societies, reform movements, and revolutionary associations. It was the city that gave birth, in the late nineteenth century, to the cheap daily newspaper, which thereafter helped mold public opinion on political and social issues. . . .

. . . To many men of the time, material progress indicated human progress, and this belief itself functioned as a religion. They were convinced that scientific advances and improved living standards were steps toward a higher civilization and the general improvement of mankind, and that in time all human problems could be solved and all abuses eliminated. Faith in human progress, joined with the strong emphasis on good works in many of the popular religious movements of the period, did much to make the nineteenth century a humanitarian age. . . .

The Norton History of Modern Europe ed. F. Gilbert (New York, 1970) pp.1037–1039

Answer the following questions:

1. Were you aware that no *purpose* for reading had been given, no specific task that indicated what information you were looking for? Do you usually establish purposes in your reading? Do you vary your reading speed and method accordingly?

2. In what ways would your reading have been altered by the following instructions:
   (a) Find out about the effects of industry on workers' standards of living.
   (b) Discover the main changes in the European economy of this time.
   (c) Find out about:
       (i) people's diet;
       (ii) daily newspapers;
       (iii) religion.

3. How much of what you read was familiar to you—terminology, people, places, general developments? Have you made a note of some kind that reminds you to research the blank spots further?

4. How much of the historical information were you able to actually visualise—the physical appearance of people, the towns, the landscape, etc?

Now read through the sections on 'Some General Principles' and 'Speeds and Gears'. Then review your answers to 1–4.

A. SOME GENERAL PRINCIPLES

Gain a Proper Perspective

A new book or topic in history is best approached by moving *from the general to the particular*, and *from the simple text to the complex one*. At the very extremes of this process, it means moving from a cursory skimming of a book in order to establish its relevance to your needs, and its scholarly stature, to a detailed appraisal of an historian's interpretation of a particular point. In this way information about both the book and the historical subject can be selected and absorbed *progressively*. You are in effect trying to gain an *overall perspective* on the whole book or topic, as well as its constituent parts. The man who wishes to move quickly through a dense forest towards a house in the middle (in the absence of a well-trodden path) takes advantage of simple maps and surrounding hills to spy out the quickest route.

Be Active

Approach all types of historical reading in an *alert, responsive and critical manner*. Analytical reading is active and not passive. You must continually *assimilate new information into the context of your earlier knowledge*. Learning to see relevant relationships like this is one of your fundamental tasks. Try to anticipate what the historian is about to say. Always be willing to ask questions of the material and demand to know more than the text is willing to divulge about people, places and events. Be prepared to reflect upon and discuss difficult or controversial points in your reading. In other words, you must try to interact with your text, as in a dialogue between people.

Be Purposeful and Flexible

You should not approach all history books in the same way. You must be clear in your mind from the very outset why you are reading. Sometimes this will be decided by your teacher/lecturer. At other times you will need to define the task for yourself—to get background information on a new topic? to research an essay question? to discover what the historian feels about a particular problem/person/event? to have a quiet read? This definition of your task will determine both the speed at which you read the historical information and the quantity of it that you will need to refer to.

In the same way, you should be willing to vary your reading speed according to the difficulty of the ideas and language in particular passages. Some books, or certain sections within the same book, are simply more difficult to grasp. Remember, however, that the difficulty of the text is relative to your existing knowledge and level of understanding of the topic. This should improve with time and study!

Be Imaginative

Try to visualise the meaning of historical writing and thereby make the past come to life. All historical writings, even those which deal with complicated and abstract ideas, narrate stories about people and their lives. Obviously not all historical writings will lend themselves to this imagining. Some texts require a far more incisive and rational approach. For instance, compare the extracts on pages 9 and 15. A great deal of pleasure and interest is lost if the reader is not able to form mental pictures of what is being referred to, however fleetingly. This facility requires a certain amount of sensitivity on your part but most certainly also needs to be developed through practice and attentiveness to details in the historical text. Do you see the people in your mind's eye—their facial expressions? the colour of their clothes? Can you hear the noises of the scene described? Have you made efforts to discover what early modern towns looked like and what the landscape's appearance might be? Prints, maps and recent photographs (of buildings and paintings, for instance), should be sought out and consulted.

| EXERCISE | BREEDING-GROUNDS FOR REVOLUTION |

Read the extract below. It attempts to make an important connection between social conditions and the origins of political revolution. But, even if you are willing to *accept* the connection, do you fully *understand* it?

'The revolutions of 1848 were, in origin and impetus, the work of towns. . . . The towns experienced a declining standard of life and a phase of acute hardship and unemployment. The conditions bred the revolutionary spirit and provided the concentration of numbers and strength which a revolutionary movement needed in order to challenge established authority.'
D. Thomson, *Europe Since Napoleon* (Harmondsworth, 1977) p. 230

Now study the contemporary photograph and engraving.

1. In what ways do they help you identify some of the specific elements in the proposed connection between town-conditions and revolution?

2. What other information does the print give you about people of this period?

A Newcastle slum.
Source: *R. J. Cootes, Britain Since 1700,* (London, 1968) p. 191. Radio Times Hulton Picture Library.

Concentrate

From the beginning of your study of History it is vital that you try to read widely and according to the principles described above. Analytical reading requires good levels of concentration, however. You must learn to be aware not only of the degrees of concentration that are possible (compare, for instance, your attention to the gripping climax of a movie with your first glances at the pages of the morning newspaper) but also of the possibility of improving your own levels of concentration. Be aware of your concentration level while reading. Pull yourself up when it lessens. Be positive and determined, and establish disciplined routines.

Problems with concentration?

SOME CAUSES	SOME SOLUTIONS
LACK OF PURPOSE	1. Define your task and actively seek out the relevant information. Take pleasure in ruthlessly ignoring irrelevant information! 2. Consult your teacher about what needs to be gained from reading about a particular topic.
LACK OF INTEREST	3. Approach the text in a more critical and/or imaginative manner. 4. Dull topics (e.g. Metternich's system) can be made more interesting by viewing them in wider, more intriguing contexts (e.g. the conflict between forces of change and continuity). 5. Challenge yourself to complete reading in fixed periods of time (but be realistic about the schedules you adopt!). 6. Reward yourself for meeting self-imposed targets or completing assignments (cups of tea, going out etc.).
FATIGUE AND DISTRACTIONS	7. Discover your optimum time for reading/study—it varies from person to person (early morning? afternoon? late at night?). 8. Ensure your physical environment is conducive to serious analytical reading—quiet, warm and well-lit. 9. Take regular breaks (about every 20–30 minutes) for short periods (usually 5 minutes is enough—no longer). 10. Learn to recognise the signs of fatigue (slight eye-ache, mind-wandering, etc.).

Analytical reading of history texts should never permit a passive acceptance of other people's interpretations of the past. Fundamentally it requires a dialogue between you, as reader and apprentice-historian, and the author, as writer and professional historian. As much as anything else it is this room for rational argument and passionate controversy which gives the study of History such colour, interest and value. The sooner you enter this world the greater will your enthusiasm for the subject be and the deeper your understanding of the past, the discipline of History and, ultimately, yourself.

B. SPEEDS AND GEARS

Reading is a very complex process. Some history students cope with it more easily and at greater speeds than others. All students, however, can learn how to use their reading speed strategically.

EXERCISE

READING ONE:
Read the extract on p.15 at your normal speed.

READING TWO:
Now read the source again to discover the following information:

(a) How many Russian exiles were on the train with Lenin?

(b) What anthem was played in Petrograd?

(c) What was Lenin wearing on his head?

READING THREE:
Read the extract on pp.20–1 in order to explain Britain's declining influence in Europe.

Discuss your reading experiences with a fellow student (e.g. difficulties with comprehension, slow reading speeds etc.).

Your three separate readings should have been executed at very different speeds, the third reading being the slowest and the second the fastest. This should have been a deliberate policy on your part. Analytical reading demands that you vary your speed of reading according to:

(a) the difficulty of the material.

(b) your exact purpose in reading it.

These two considerations are closely connected. The third reading, for instance, was slower than the first, despite the fact that you knew exactly what you were looking for. Why?

Because:
(a) comprehension is the most important aspect of your history reading. If necessary, therefore, difficult passages need to be read over and over until you have understood them.

(b) proper definition of the purposes in reading will help you to know how much you need to understand. Some tasks are simpler than others (compare the third and second readings for instance).

Consult the chart for a general idea of how reading speed (usually calculated in words per minute) relates to:

(a) ranges of speed (as 'gears' in a car).

(b) levels of comprehension (which will inevitably fall as reading speed increases, depending on material).

The chart will be of greater value if you calculate your own normal reading speed and then adjust the relationship between reading speeds and 'gears' accordingly.

$$\text{Reading speed (w.p.m.)} = \frac{\text{No. of pages read} \times \text{No. of words per average page}}{\text{No. of minutes spent reading}}$$

Average Standard	Speed (w.p.m.)	'Gear'	Expected Comprehension %	Purpose (and Difficulty of Material)
Slow	Less than 50	Crawl	100	Careful Studying (Very Difficult)
	100	Coasting	70–80	Reading for Meaning/ Pleasure/Information etc. (Easy/Normal Material)
Normal	200			
	300			
Fast	400	Racing	below 50	1. 'Overview' Skimming 2. Revision Learning: 1st stage of review
	500			
Exceptionally fast	600	Blur	below 10	1. 'Scanning' for Specific Words 2. Author's Arrangement of His Material and Ideas
	700			
	800			
	900			
	1000			
	up to			
	3000			

C. HISTORY BOOKS

Their Variety

You will soon discover that a bewildering variety of history books have been written over several decades on the modern period alone. This is largely because historians often disagree, and sometimes fundamentally, about what happened in the past and why. The study of History at Advanced level is not merely the collection of facts about the past, but is rather the explanation and interpretation of the relationships between those facts. Historians construct their own personal picture of past events (a) on the basis of their interpretation of primary sources (which they use as 'evidence' to support their own viewpoint) and (b) through their reliance on earlier historians' work in the field of study (i.e. secondary sources). They attempt, as far as possible, to base their interpretations upon factual evidence from primary sources, but still they often disagree. There are many complex reasons for historians' disagreement.

Some of these are:

(a) There is often a lack of primary evidence. Historians must therefore bridge these gaps by intelligent and imaginative thinking.

(b) Some evidence is not fully reliable, being inaccurate and biased.

(c) The facts in History do not always speak for themselves. It is the historian who decides what facts mean, whether they are important, and which ones he is going to select as part of his interpretation. This is subjective and therefore open to disagreement.

(d) The massive body of historical research that has gone on throughout this century has gradually discovered new sources of information and refined our views of the early modern period, in all probability bringing them closer to the objective truth.

| EXERCISE | LLOYD GEORGE'S REPUTATION

In the twenty-nine years that have passed since Lloyd George's death, he has continued to stir up furious argument amongst historians and biographers. Many of the latter—for instance Thomas Jones, whose biography appeared in 1951—were generally sympathetic, even if their enthusiasm was somewhat guarded. But the dominant tendency in the interpretations of Lloyd George's career until the mid-1960s was overwhelmingly critical. Writers of varying political persuasions unsparingly heaped condemnation on his private and public life. . . . Almost every major work of scholarship written in the past six or seven years on recent British political history has taken a far more balanced view of him than seemed likely at the time of his death. At last he may be turning into a credible historical figure, capable of being understood, even admired.

To an astonishing degree, the controversy about him has taken the form of a continuing debate about his private life. The sexual proclivities of no other prime minister have aroused quite the same kind of obsessive inquiry. . . .

Now that new evidence, either not released before or else wilfully ignored by earlier historians, is available, these charges can be reduced to their proper perspective. Now that we have in print the diary of his second wife, and his correspondence with Dame Margaret, Lloyd George's private morality can be viewed in historical terms. It is quite obvious that the image of an unbridled libertine is a total myth: Lloyd George was above all the complete professional politician dedicated to public objectives, not to private lust. . . .

. . . As Professor John Vincent has cogently written, 'Lloyd George's best-kept secret is out—respectability'.

Other charges also made about his character will also have to be modified. It has often been alleged that he was incapable of friendship; that he was ruthless and unforgiving in sacrificing associates. 'He had no friends and did not deserve any,' A.J.P. Taylor once wrote. F.S. Oliver had written of Lloyd George years before, 'He does not understand what friendship means.' In fact, Lloyd George was a man with profound human qualities.

K.O. Morgan, *Lloyd George* (London, 1974) pp.200, 201, 205

1. What evidence can you find which supports the idea that historical knowledge has improved with time? Does it necessarily follow that it will? Give reasons for your answer.

2. Over which points have historians disagreed in their interpretations?

Finding your way through the wood

Make use of all kinds of history books. Historians have different purposes when writing their books. They may be trying to understand and explain a whole period of the past or they may be concentrating on one individual problem. Move *from the general to the specific* and from the *simple to the complex*. Look for the wood before the trees!

GENERAL HISTORIES:

These are based largely on existing historical studies and usually offer a good overview of a period or topic. They are by nature general syntheses and should be used firstly and mainly as an introduction to a topic. The best of these general histories offer a coherent and original interpretation of the subject matter.

e.g. D. Thomson, *Europe Since Napoleon* (1977)
A.J.P. Taylor, *The Struggle for Mastery in Europe, 1848–1918* (1971)
J.M. Roberts, *Europe 1880–1945* (1967)

Others are less original but can provide excellent introductions to historical topics and issues.

MONOGRAPHS:

These are specialised and, usually, original interpretations of major topics based upon detailed, extensive researching of primary sources. This is 'front line' historical work with a narrow focus. It is very valuable to you since it will be detailed and original, may criticise other historians' views and will provide a good insight into the wide range of sources that historians must consult before they are able to offer convincing interpretations (see their use of footnotes and consult the bibliographies).

e.g. M. Cowling, *Disraeli, Gladstone and Revolution* (1967)
R. Conquest, *The Great Terror* (1968)
S. Constantine, *Unemployment in Britain between the Wars* (1980)

JOURNALS AND PAMPHLETS:

When historians are working on major pieces of research, or wish to deal with other historians' views on particular topics, they may contribute articles to historical journals as interim reports on their work in progress. They are useful to you since:

(a) the articles are relatively brief and succinct (anything from 3 to 30 pages).

(b) they offer examples of the most up-to-date work on historical subjects.

(c) the Journals' book reviews can keep you up-to-date with recent work on your period and give you a flavour of historical criticism and debate.

Some of the most useful and renowned journals for the modern period are listed below. They appear quarterly, available to the subscriber or in bound copies at central reference libraries:

Past and Present
English Historical Review
Historical Journal

Economic History Review
American Historical Review

How might this advice work out in practice? Let us apply the principle of moving from the general/simple to the specialist/complex to a specific example:

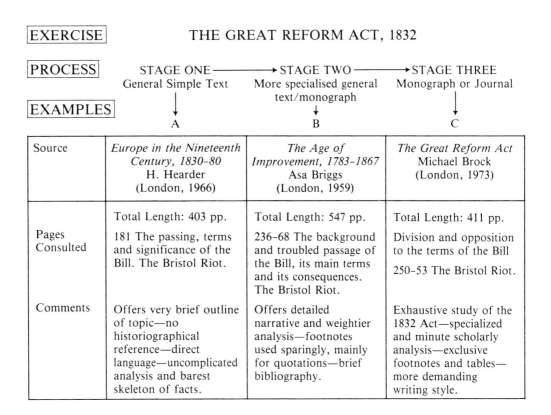

EXERCISE — THE GREAT REFORM ACT, 1832

PROCESS — STAGE ONE → STAGE TWO → STAGE THREE
General Simple Text | More specialised general text/monograph | Monograph or Journal

EXAMPLES — A | B | C

Source	*Europe in the Nineteenth Century, 1830-80* H. Hearder (London, 1966)	*The Age of Improvement, 1783-1867* Asa Briggs (London, 1959)	*The Great Reform Act* Michael Brock (London, 1973)
Pages Consulted	Total Length: 403 pp. 181 The passing, terms and significance of the Bill. The Bristol Riot.	Total Length: 547 pp. 236-68 The background and troubled passage of the Bill, its main terms and its consequences. The Bristol Riot.	Total Length: 411 pp. Division and opposition to the terms of the Bill 250-53 The Bristol Riot.
Comments	Offers very brief outline of topic—no historiographical reference—direct language—uncomplicated analysis and barest skeleton of facts.	Offers detailed narrative and weightier analysis—footnotes used sparingly, mainly for quotations—brief bibliography.	Exhaustive study of the 1832 Act—specialized and minute scholarly analysis—exclusive footnotes and tables—more demanding writing style.

SOME HINTS

Stages 1 and 2 of the process will usually be sufficient for most topics. Stage 3 is recommended only for research topics (e.g. special study options, or extended essays) or out of personal interest in a particular topic.

—*Read as many major works of interpretation as possible.* At the very least you should consult two historians whose views you know to be opposed or at variance.

—*Learn to study footnotes* for further information and as clues to the scholarship and plausibility of the historian's arguments. Few general texts, but most monographs, use footnotes—either at the bottom of the page or at the back of the chapter/book. *The validity of historians' views are largely determined by the evidence upon which they are claimed to be based.* It is demanded by academic standards therefore that a historian should acknowledge his source of significant pieces of information—facts and interpretations:

(a) To indicate the validity of the factual evidence (i.e. where is it from?)

(b) To acknowledge indebtedness to the researches and writings of other historians (i.e. how original is a particular view?)

(c) To develop points in the main text and to recommend/criticise other historical writings on particular points.

EXTRACTS

A

The Reform Bill crisis lasted for fifteen months. Two Bills were defeated and before the third was passed Grey was obliged to dissolve the House, fight a general election and engage in a fierce struggle with the House of Lords. Furious reform agitation spread from Birmingham, where Thomas Attwood's 'Political Union of the Lower and Middle Classes of the People' had been founded in 1829, to London and the south. There were mass disturbances in the winter of 1830–31, reaching a climax in a considerable mob rising in Bristol. The eventual passing of the Bill in June 1832 was greeted with rejoicing throughout the country. By extending the franchise and redistributing seats, the 1832 Act increased the electorate by almost exactly a half. Both reformers and opponents had expected a more striking change in the size of the electorate but in so far as it introduced a new class to political influence the Great Reform Act deserves to be considered a revolution no less — and perhaps more — than do the events of 1830 in Paris.

B

The Whigs, exclusive and aristocratic though they were in their attitude to government, were ready to accept political innovations. Indeed, they believed that unless the privileged sections of the community were prepared to adapt and to 'improve', waves of dangerous and uncontrollable innovation would completely drown the existing social order. While their opponents in 1830 believed that a considerable measure of parliamentary reform would lead to national catastrophe, the Whigs maintained that only a considerable measure could prevent a catastrophe. . . .

Whigs and Tories were agreed during the crucial debates of 1830–32 that democracy was an unpalatable and dangerous form of government, that 'a stake in the country' was an essential title to political power, that landed property had a special part to play in guaranteeing the stability of the social order and the authority of the Constitution, that the 'wild' — as distinct from the 'rational' — part of the public should not be left undisturbed to exercise pressure on governmental policy. The Whigs, however, were responsive to some of the movements of change and responsible in relation to the rest. There were some Whigs too who went much further than Grey in their willingness to innovate. . . .

In detail, Russell proposed completely to disfranchise small boroughs of less than 2,000 inhabitants, most of which were under the influence of a particular local patron, and some of which, like Old Sarum, were green mounds or heaps of stone. He went on to propose the semi-disfranchisement of a second group of small boroughs with a population of under 4,000, allowing each borough one instead of two members. Of the 168 vacancies thus created, 42 were to be filled by new borough seats, including eight new London seats and seats for Manchester, Leeds, and Birmingham; 55 were to be devoted to the provision of additional members for countries, to augment what had traditionally been regarded as the most 'independent' element in the representative system; and nine new places were to be given to Scotland, Ireland and Wales. The remaining vacancies were not to be filled at all, so that the new House of Commons was to be significantly smaller than the old. As far as the conditions of voting were concerned, the 40s. freehold vote was to be retained in the counties, but in the boroughs the vote was everywhere to be offered to the £10 householder, the man who occupied — either as owner or tenant of one landlord — buildings of an annual value of £10. The 'real property' and 'the real respectability' of the new centres of population would thus be given political weight, and the national electorate would be enlarged by 'about half a million persons, and these all connected with the property of the country, having a valuable stake amongst us, and deeply interested in our institutions'. . . .

There was rioting and arson at Nottingham and Derby, Worcester and Bath, and finally on 29 October the city centre at Bristol was sacked by an angry mob in the worst riots of the year. The words 'liberty' and 'slavery' which had frequently been on the lips of the Bristol slavery abolitionists were taken up by the crowds, and the weakness of both mayor and military left the mob free to do much as it wished.

C

Professor D.C. Moore has lately questioned how far the Bill was, or was ever thought to be, a concession by the aristocracy.[85] A life-long reformer such as Russell clearly saw himself, not as conceding, but as strengthening aristocratic influence. Melbourne, on the other hand, put a higher value on what was being surrendered. But this does not mean that Melbourne saw the Bill as a gratuitous concession. If inaction is believed to involve losing the whole, to promote a change which is aimed, on a low estimate, at keeping three-quarters does not imply an intention of conceding a great deal. The aristocracy may not have done as well out of the change as its authors planned. But a very small Reform, or none at all, would—or, at least, might—have involved the aristocrats in far larger losses and concessions than any which they incurred through the Reform Act. Lady Elizabeth Belgrave's comment, when the government's scheme was first published, probably indicates the predominant reaction among the whig borough owners. Lady Elizabeth was the Marquess of Stafford's younger daughter and had married the heir to the Grosvenor interest. 'This will clip the aristocracy,' she wrote to her mother, 'but a good deal must be sacrificed to save the rest.'[86] . . .

Divisive though the national guard proposals might be, the *Morning Chronicle* took them up, and, being friendlier than the *Globe* to the radicals, did so with less of a repressive, middle-class twist. On 26 October the *Chronicle* called for a National Guard which would unite 'the most respectable and efficient of the middle and labouring classes'. On the following day *The Times* demanded the formation of 'Conservative Guards' who were to be drawn from 'the whole mass of householders'. They 'should be drilled occasionally and taught the use of the firelock'.

The pleas for conservative guards might have died away had it not been for the Bristol riots which broke out on 29 October and raged for three days. Bristol was a turbulent port containing all the ingredients for a riot. The corporation was self-elected and of the weakest kind. Although it had contained a tory majority since 1812 the mayor was a reformer. . . . .

Wetherell reached the Mansion House safely on 29 October. But a riot developed outside in Queen's Square. The sessions were postponed and he escaped over the roof. Next morning the Mansion House was stormed and sacked and the mobs increased until they were some thousands strong. The military commander, Lieutenant Colonel Brereton, failed to obtain support from the magistrates and withdrew two of his troops from the city. An appeal from the Political Union had no effect on the rioters. By daylight on 31 October two sides of Queen's Square, including the Custom House and Excise Office, together with the Bishop's Palace and several gaols and toll houses, had been pillaged and burned.

Brereton was court-martialled for his performance in the riots and shot himself before the case had ended. . . . .

| QUESTIONS |

1. What clues do the source information, length of book, date of publication and length of discussion give you about the nature of the different writings?

2. Compare extract A and B.
   (a) How far are they in *agreement* in their analysis of the topic?
   (b) In what ways does extract B *add* to your understanding of the topic provided in A?

3. Compare extracts A, B and C.
   (a) Would it have mattered if the sequence in our process had been altered (e.g. B, C, A or C, B, A)?
   (b) Read p.10 again.? Although the 3 extracts above are necessarily brief do they illustrate the differences pointed to on p.10? Give specific examples.

FORMAT

(1) Historian's Name (2) Title of Work (3) Publication Details (e.g. volume or edition number or series title or place and date of publication) (4) page number.

Examples from Extract C above

85. D. C. Moore, 'Concession or Cure: the Sociological Premises of the First Reform Act', *Hist. Journal*, ix (1966), 39–59. See also Professor Moore's articles in *Victorian Studies*, v (1961), 7–34; xiii (1969), 5–36; xiv (1971), 328–37—reply to Dr E. P. Hennock; *Ideas and Institutions of Victorian Britain*, Ed. R. Robson (1967), pp. 20–57. These articles are of great interest, though some of the views in them have been controverted.

86. G. Huxley, *Lady Elizabeth and the Grosvenors* (1965), p. 98.

ABBREVIATIONS

(These are only the most commonly used.)

c. (or ca.)	about (as in a date)
cf.	compare with
ed(s)	editor(s) or edition(s)
ff.	following or onwards
Ibid.	in the same place
MS(S)	manuscript(s)
op.(loc. cit.)	in the work(place) already cited
passim	throughout
pp.	pages
q.v.	which see (as in a recommended work)
ser.	series (of journals)
v.	volume

Build up your own personal library—as far as your budget will allow! Most important historical books are available in paperback and will repay constant reference. You can often re-sell books and cut the original cost of purchase.

Learn to use the library efficiently for both study and reference. Make a habit of consulting several works when researching topics and essays. Learn to browse, seeking out unfamiliar authors and new books alike.

History books can usually be found under the following classification systems:

Library of Congress		D.D.C.	
D.	General History	930	History in General
D.A.	Great Britain	940	History of Europe
20–690	England	941	Britain
700–745	Wales	941.1	Scotland
750–800	Scotland	941.5	Ireland
900–995	Ireland	943	Germany
DB	Austro-Hungary		
DC	France		
DD	Germany		

LIBRARY ⇨

Their Structure

THE TYPES OF HISTORICAL WRITING

Your own historical writing and thinking will be expected to distinguish between fact and interpretation and between statements of a descriptive rather than an analytical kind.

It is important therefore that you learn to distinguish between different kinds of historical writings, since these will be your major source of information about the modern period.

It is possible to identify three main types of historical writing—descriptive, narrative and analytical. All three types combine facts and interpretations but differ in terms of:

(a) their relative emphasis on these elements.

(b) the language they use.

(c) the complexity of their conceptual thinking.

A. DESCRIPTIVE HISTORY: *LENIN'S RETURN FROM EXILE*

In the train that left in the morning of April 8 there were thirty Russian exiles, including not a single Menshevik . . . Some of the best of the comrades had been horrified by the indiscretion of Lenin in resorting to the aid of the Germans and making the trip through an enemy country. They came to the station and besieged the travellers, begging them not to go. Lenin got into the train without replying a word. In the carriage he found a comrade, who had been suspected of being a stool-pigeon. 'The man had made a little too sure of his seat. Suddenly we saw Lenin seize him by the collar and in an incomparable matter-of-fact manner pitch him out on to the platform.' . . .

. . . the train got in very late the night of April 16. On the platform he (Lenin) had been confronted by men come back from from prison or exile, who greeted him with tears on their cheeks . . .

On the platform outside, an officer came up and saluted. Lenin, surprised, returned the salute. The officer gave the command: a detachment of sailors with bayonets stood at attention. The place was being spotted by searchlight and bands were playing the Marseillaise. A great roar of a cheer went up from a crowd that was pressing all around. 'What's this?' Lenin said, stepping back. They told him it was a welcome to Petrograd by the revolutionary workers and sailors: they had been roaring one word—'Lenin'. The sailors presented arms, and their commander reported to Lenin for duty. It was whispered that they wanted him to speak. He walked a few paces and took off his bowler hat . . .

(Later) They wanted to give Lenin tea and to treat him to speeches of welcome, but he made them talk about tactics. The palace was surrounded by a crowd who were shouting for him to speak. He went out on a balcony to meet them. It was as if all the stifled rebellion on which the great flat and heavy city had pressed with its pompous facades since the time of those artisans whom Peter the Great had sent to perish in building it in the swamp, had boiled up in a single night. And Lenin, who had talked only at party meetings, before audiences of Marxist students, who had hardly appeared in public in 1905, now spoke to them with a voice of authority that was to pick up all their undirected energy, to command their uncertain confidence, and to swell suddenly to a world-wide resonance.

Edmund Wilson, *To the Finland Station* (N.Y., 1964) pp.464, 468, 470, 472.

QUESTIONS

1. Writings of this kind concentrate on presenting a visual image or impression of a person, idea or event. In your own words describe the image that this extract gives.

2. To discover the main points in this writing you must identify the key words and phrases that create the mental picture. Make a list of such main points.

3. Descriptive writing is composed of statements of fact and interpretation. Find examples of each in the extract.

B. NARRATIVE HISTORY: *THE ANTI-CORN LAW, LEAGUE*

Only with the Conservative ministry of Sir Robert Peel from 1841 to 1846 did the great switch to a *laissez-faire* policy begin on a broader scale. By 1841 the movement for free trade in the country had centred on an attack on the Corn Laws. In their most unpopular form the Corn Laws dated from 1815 when they had imposed a high tariff on imported corn to protect home-grown corn in freak economic conditions. A group of parliamentary radicals founded on Anti-Corn Law Association in London in 1836 to demand total repeal of the tariff, and in 1838 a similar and more effective body was formed in Manchester. The next year it was renamed the Anti-Corn Law League. For the first years of the Whig period after The Reform Act of 1832, the government's financial policies had seemed successful, but a change for the worse was now taking place. There was a bad deficit in 1838. The price of bread rose steeply. The number of paupers grew. Lancashire was experiencing a grim depression. In these circumstances, the Anti-Corn law movement fell into the able hands of Richard Cobden.

H. Hearder, *Europe in the Nineteenth Century* (London, 1966) p.96

QUESTIONS

1. The predominant motive for writing this type of history is to demonstrate chronological sequence. You must be aware of the principal events and characters in the story. What are the key points in the extract?

2. Narrative is a form of explanation. The historian must first personally select the facts that he presents in his narrative because he cannot include them all. He therefore must omit information.

    (a) From your reading of the extract, why do you think that the historian has selected only these particular facts for his narrative?

    (b) From your knowledge of the reign, which other facts (i) could have been included, (ii) would have altered the nature of the narrative?

3. Find examples where the historian has blended facts with (a) interpretation, (b) personal opinion.

C. ANALYTICAL HISTORY: *EUROPE'S RULING CLASS*

Around the turn of the century the prevalent form of government in Europe was the monarchy. There were only two republics: France and Switzerland. The degree to which monarchial rulers possessed concrete political power varied. But whether or not they had sufficient power to exert real influence on state policy, the monarchs were justified in considering themselves the most important persons on the European political stage. In each country the monarch was the apex of society, and the status of both individuals and groups was dependent on their relationship to the throne. Among themselves, royalty formed a kind of gigantic family which seemed to tie European society together into one great unit. . . .

The monarchs were also the leaders of the society in their respective countries. In holding court they reinforced a traditional hierarchy and determined its order by giving titles and decorations and by receiving or excluding people according to the standards of the crown. . . .

. . . The existence of a monarchy presupposed the existence of a ruling group closely connected with the throne. In the eighteenth century the princes of continental Europe had become absolute by gaining direct control of the armed forces and by allying themselves with the landowning nobility. This alliance of the monarchs with the army and the landed aristocracy lasted into the twentieth century. Although by that time an elected parliament had become an influential factor in politics, the arbiter of social status remained the court, with its officialdom of ministers, chamberlains, masters of ceremonies—all nobles and mostly descendants of the oldest families. The monarchs kept up their special closeness to the army by insisting on a voice in the promotion of officers. . . .

The eminence of a landed aristocracy, which had been justified by the economic and political conditions of previous centuries, seemed an anomaly in the twentieth century, when industry and commerce became dominating factors in economic life. The heads of the large banks, the owners and managers of the great industrial enterprises, were the creators of the prosperity and power of a nation. But even in those countries in which industrialization was most advanced, agriculture still retained an important place in the economy. . . .

There remained differences, however, between the industrial and agricultural sectors of European society, and these differences were most clearly reflected in the bourgeois advocacy of free trade and the aristocratic demand for tariffs. Moreover, the less well-situated members of the nobility looked with envy and disdain on the increasing wealth of the bourgeoisie. The owners of smaller industrial enterprises usually retained many of the antiaristocratic views of the early nineteenth century, when the bourgeoisie had been struggling against the Old Regime. Yet, between the upper strata of the landed aristocracy and the wealthiest members of the industrial and commercial society there were many links; and gradually these two elements came to be joined together in a single ruling group. . . .

Authoritarian concepts and aristocratic mores and interests pervaded the thinking and the aims of the owners and managers of industry. And the dominance among them of this point of view hardened the tensions and conflicts within an industrial society.

F. Gilbert et. al., *Modern Europe* (N.Y., 1971) pp.1234–9

By far the most common and most difficult type of historical writing is that which seeks to lay bare the 'true nature' of an event. This analytical writing may also involve elements of description and narration. It is essentially concerned, however, with discovering the real causes and nature of historical events as well as the thoughts, attitudes and emotions that motivated individuals in the past.

Historical explanation is, for you, the most important aspect of this type of writing. It is essential therefore, that you identify and appreciate the historian's viewpoint, follow the individual steps in his arguments and pinpoint the specific reasons he offers for his views.

QUESTIONS

1. In what order has the historian above decided to analyse the question of a ruling group in Europe? What reasons can you offer for this order?

2. What is his main view or conclusion on this question?

WHAT IS THE BOOK ABOUT?

History books have their main ideas, supporting evidence and factual details arranged in a particular manner. There are individual differences, but all history books tend to organise information in an hierarchical way. This is unfolded gradually from 'top to bottom'. The diagram below illustrates this point.

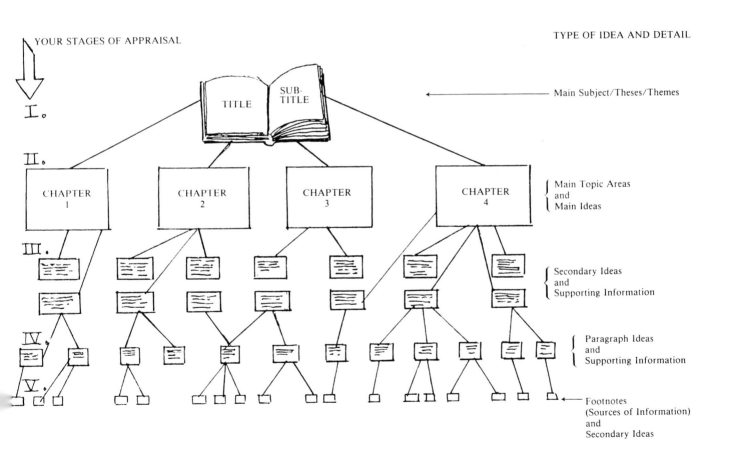

YOUR STAGES OF APPRAISAL

TYPE OF IDEA AND DETAIL

I.

II.

III.

IV.

V.

TITLE SUB-TITLE

CHAPTER 1   CHAPTER 2   CHAPTER 3   CHAPTER 4

Main Subject/Theses/Themes

Main Topic Areas and Main Ideas

Secondary Ideas and Supporting Information

Paragraph Ideas and Supporting Information

Footnotes (Sources of Information) and Secondary Ideas

I.

A SIMPLIFIED EXAMPLE

THE ANARCHISTS	RODERICK KEDWARD (London, 1971) 128pp

The men who shocked an era

II.

1. THE MAKING OF AN ANARCHIST

1. From 1880–1918 the Anarchist movement was at its height. Its members violently protested against the authoritarian values and organizations of bourgeois society. They opposed the widespread social injustice of the industrial age.

2. Although partly based on the earlier theories of Pierre Proudhon and Michael Bakunin anarchist thought and action was very diverse, mainly as a result of its individualism and social origins.

3. COLLECTIVE REVOLT

1. Intellectuals like Kropotkin spread the idea that wholesale revolution and anarchy was imminent, certain and right. A model of collective revolt was discovered in the Paris Commune of 1871 with its moral idealism and local political autonomy.

2. Anarchy had a significant impact on revolutionary trade unionism (syndicalism) in France, Spain and Italy, and played a troubled role in the Bolshevik revolution in Russia.

5. MYTH AND REALITY

1. Anarchism lay outside the mainstream of events: a violent and idealistic side-show on the margins of history.

2. Anarchism did provide an important analysis of contemporary social values and injustices.

2. INDIVIDUAL TERROR

1. 'Propaganda by deed' was accepted by anarchists as an appropriate method of protest and revenge. Violence was seen as the midwife of social change.

2. Society mistakenly (a) branded all anarchists as evil and subhuman because of the creed's random, violent nature, and (b) accepted the myth of an international anarchist plot.

4. FREEDOM AND ANARCHY

1. Anarchism became a highly developed creed of individual freedom and creative innovation, opposed to ignorance, moral prejudice and cultural orthodoxy.

2. Some anarchists made positive moves towards establishing new forms of education and cultural expression.

III. & IV

1. 'The great age of the anarchists in Europe and America lay between 1880 and 1914 . . . The anarchists were no less dynamic, inventive, and imaginative than their age . . . Their mobility was a scourge to the police of all countries, their sensational actions stole the headlines of the press and their philosophy of struggle and revolt outstripped all rival doctrines of change.' (5)

2. 'The only way to equality and justice they believed was to destroy all traces of authority and to build a society without government . . . Beyond this the anarchists produced a wealth of disagreement. No single coherent programme of anarchism emerged . . . it remained a collection of different emotions, ideas and actions . . .' (6)

3. 'Violence in the late nineteenth century became the most spontaneous and dramatic of the anarchists' answers: society was to be transformed by assassination, bombs, and individual acts of terrorism . . . (but) the terrorists were seen to be marginal figures, isolated on the fringe of the anarchist movements.' (13–14)

4. 'The purpose was to be morally independent and to think for oneself, rationally and without prejudice.' (16)

5. '. . . anarchist trade unionism, known as anarcho-syndicalism, was forged in the heat of economic and class division . . . (it) aimed to transform society by means of strikes, in particular the general strike, mounted as a revolutionary action by all workers and ushering in the age of freedom and justice.' (17)

6. 'In the first place, most of the terrorists were products of social, economic or personal misery and, secondly, most of them were solitary figures determined to preserve their independence.' (24)

These six secondary ideas in chapter 1 are distilled from a detailed discussion over many pages.

This structure of ideas is sometimes very difficult to discover (especially at Stages III and IV). Nonetheless it is important that you learn to break history books down into their original skeletal form.

THE SILENT DIALOGUE

Look at the diagram below. It provides a simple model that shows the unspoken conversation that should go on between you and the historian through the medium of the history book. Ultimately you (R) are involved in a reverse process of what the historian (H) underwent while writing the book.

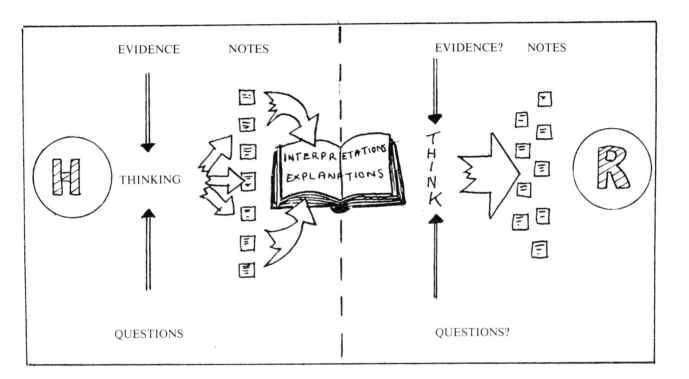

HINTS SOME READER'S QUESTIONS

What are the historian's central arguments/themes throughout the book/chapter/pamphlet/article? What questions is he trying to answer?

In what subject/topic areas does he discuss these?

What connecting/secondary ideas does he use to develop, clarify and support his main argument?

What evidence does he cite to support his statements? How convincing is this evidence?

Some Common Problems for Readers

History books, even the most general of introductory texts, can sometimes provide problems for you (the apprentice historian and analytical reader!). *Remember that you are reading not only for historical information but also to increase your historical understanding.* It is possible for you to gain the former (knowledge of Napoleon III's rule, for instance) and not the latter (appreciating the various factors in his rise to power, the expansionist nature of his economic policy and the paternalism of his social policy, etc.

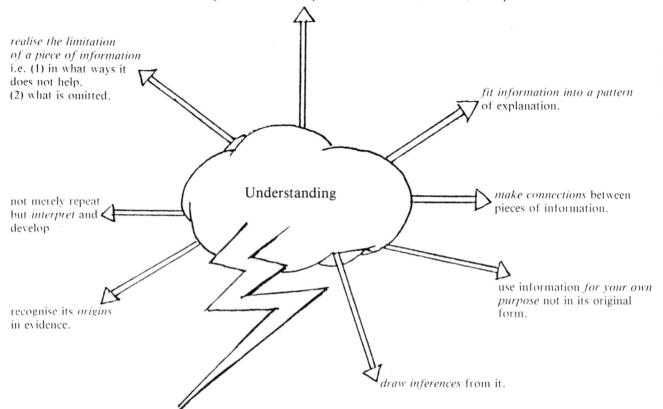

When you understand, you . . .

place a value on a piece of information, theorise, conceptualise from it.

*realise the limitation
of a piece of information*
i.e. (1) in what ways it
does not help.
(2) what is omitted.

fit information into a pattern
of explanation.

Understanding

*not merely repeat
but interpret and
develop*

make connections between
pieces of information.

*use information for your own
purpose* not in its original
form.

recognise its origins
in evidence.

draw inferences from it.

EXERCISE

Read the extract below and the discussion that follows it. Then answer the questions that refer to this extract:

BRITISH DIPLOMACY AND EUROPE, 1850–70

In the confident years after 1815 Britain's world-wide influence, buttressed by her navy and her commercial supremacy, had been acknowledged on every side. In the 1850s and 1860s, however, just as the domestic tranquillity which accompanies prosperity was achieved, the first significant blows to Britain's 'power of prestige'
5   were struck. Britain, the self-assured Palmerston included, reacted too slowly to shifts in the balance of forces in Europe after 1848 and found her power to influence Continental affairs substantially reduced. In the wider world, though Britain's trading primacy remained universally recognized, perplexing questions of commercial influence and colonial domination presented themselves. Increased defence commit-
10 ments were required. According to the classical canons of Gladstonian Liberalism, economic *laissez-faire* implied minimal government interference and the lowest taxes possible. Yet in 1869, the first full year of Gladstone's prime ministership, Britain spent £27m. on her army and navy, virtually twice as much as when Palmerston gave his advice to Malmesbury. Britain's world role did not come on the cheap and
15   Gladstone would never realize his dearest ambition, to abolish the income tax.

Fear of Russia preoccupied British statesmen until the end of the 1850s. Attention still concentrated on the Black Sea and on the slow subsidence of the Turkish Empire from which, it was believed, Russia alone would gain, with consequent hazard to British strategic and commercial interests. The area was increasingly important

20 because British trade with the Turks increased eight-fold in the 1830s and 1840s.
    Perhaps the single most important misjudgement of Palmerston's career was his failure to anticipate Prussia's drive to dominate the North German states. Bismarck exposed Palmerston's boast when he annexed Schleswig and Holstein in 1864 amid anguished but inconsequential talk of British intervention. British embarrassment was
25 the greater since only the previous year the Prince of Wales had married Alexandra, daughter of the King of Denmark. Family ties, however, did not prevent Victoria's clear-headed assessment that intervention was useless. The incident weakened British claims to be considered a powerful ally in European affairs. The next year von Moltke, one of the architects of Prussia's military revival, remarked contemptuously
30 but not inaccurately to his brother that 'England is as powerless on the Continent as she is presuming'.
    In fact, in the five years after Palmerston's death in 1865, Britain 'presumed' less and less. She stood aside from the Austro-Prussian War and watched while Prussia completed her preparation for pan-German hegemony. Some politicians even
35 applauded this development as the most desirable counterbalance to French pre-tension. The non-interventionist Edward Stanley, Foreign Secretary in his father's Conservative government of 1866–68, stated a fortnight after taking office that 'if North Germany is to become a single great Power, I do not see that any English interest is in the least degree affected'. It proved to be one of the most spectacular diplomatic
40 misjudgements in history. Britain's only significant initiative was to guarantee Luxembourg's neutrality at an international conference held in London under Stanley's chairmanship in 1867. Napoleon III had threatened the independence of Luxembourg, thereby awakening long-established concerns about the preservation of Belgium's territorial integrity. Gladstone confirmed his government's determination
45 after 1868 not 'to assume alone an advanced, and therefore an isolated position, in regard to European controversies'. Both Conservative and Liberal governments, therefore, groped towards non-intervention and both remained convinced that France, rather than Prussia, represented the major threat. Britain was totally unpre-pared for the cataclysm of the Franco-Prussian War late in 1870 and still less for its
50 outcome.

E. J. Evans, *The Forging of the Modern State, 1783–1870* (London, 1983) pp.338–9

PROBLEM 1

DISCOVERING THE MAIN POINTS

Learn to distinguish between the main point of the history book and the main point of your reading—they may not necessarily be the same thing. History books can sometimes be written in a style that is difficult to penetrate. The text is often compact and dense with information.

Separating main ideas from subsidiary points (and both of these from supporting or qualifying information) is not always easy and requires practice, good levels of concentration and a clear definition of your reading purposes. *Your main task here is to separate the content from the presentation.* On the other hand, not all the words on the page are relevant to your understanding of the main point. *Don't be afraid to leave things out!*

SOME HINTS

The historian's main points or ideas can usually be discovered in (a) the first and/or last paragraph of a chapter or section, (b) the first sentence of a paragraph—this is the key point for the paragraph and it is usually expressed in one sentence. The historian usually has only one main point in each paragraph.

Rephrase the main point(s) in your own words once you have found it. This helps understanding and recall. Try to reduce these points into simple statements.

QUESTIONS

1. What are the historian's main points in the extract? Where are they to be found?

2. Read lines 1–15. Put the main point of the paragraph in your own words. What relation has all the rest of the information to this main point? Why has it been included? Which parts are (a) important developments of the main point (e.g. to clarify, prove or illustrate), and (b) unnecessary for your understanding of the main point?

3. Consider the following reading tasks that you may have been set, either by yourself or your teacher:
   (a) 'What were the main principles of British diplomacy during this period?' (for personal notes).
   (b) 'What factors contributed to the decline of Britain's foreign influence in the last half of the nineteenth century?' (essay title).

   (c) 'Find out about the connection between Britain's commercial interests and her foreign policy.' (for class discussion).
   Which points in lines 1–20 are relevant to each of these three tasks? Is this information the same as the historian's main paragraph point? In the whole extract which points are relevant to task (b)?

4. Study the diagram on p.28. How far does this framework of questions help you to identify the main points which relate to Britain's foreign policy in this period? What other questions does this framework raise that are not answered by the extract? Does this mean that they are not important?

PROBLEM 2

MAKING CONNECTIONS

Assuming you understand the history text, you must then relate this information into the background context of your knowledge of the subject matter. This is a crucial part of your analytical reading and a fundamental way of increasing your historical understanding. It should go on while you are reading.

SOME HINTS

Learn to be aware of all connections, even those that are only indirectly relevant (factual details, interpretations, individuals, other historians' views on issues).

Select ideas and information that are new and 'file' in your mental system (you haven't got one?!) or add to your notes.

Compare familiar ideas and information with what you already know—note differences and make judgements upon these issues.

Your main task here is constantly to review and revise your historical knowledge and understanding.

This is a process that takes time to master. It is one that, by its nature, becomes easier as your knowledge increases. In effect you are creating a context of knowledge into which all your reading must be assimilated. Sometimes historians assume when they are writing that this context already exists in the mind of the reader (e.g. that you are familiar with a particular person or idea; that you have background knowledge of a topic).

QUESTIONS

1. What seems to be assumed by the author about your prior knowledge in the following lines:
   (a) 1–2 (b) 3–5 (c) 16–19 (d) 48–50

2. Consider 16–20 again. It provides a convenient example of (a) how important contextual knowledge is and (b) how you might make the kinds of connections mentioned above.

Assume that the author provided only his opening statement about Britain's fear of Russia (line 16). The next points (16–20) expand upon the opening statement by providing explanation and illustrative detail.

(a) How meaningful would the first statement have been to you without this additional information?

(b) Which parts of this additional information could be further expanded by your own contextual knowledge?

PROBLEM 3

THE HISTORIAN'S LANGUAGE

1. ORDINARY WORDS

Historians use ordinary everyday language to communicate their thoughts but this can obstruct the historian's attempt to reveal the truth about the past:

(a) It sometimes prevents the historian from understanding his evidence. For instance, the historian uses concepts and collective nouns, (e.g. 'Fascism' and 'Fascists') to describe groups of people and ideas. But is a fascist, as some historians argue, a peculiar feature of Italy? Nazism would therefore not be 'fascist'. Or is fascism merely a form of totalitarianism? In which case Stalin would become a fascist. Some left-wing historians argue that fascism is equivalent to all capitalism. In this case Stanley Baldwin would become a fascist!

(b) It sometimes makes it difficult for the historian to communicate his precise meaning.

Metaphors, descriptive words and even nouns can lead to vagueness and ambiguity for the reader.

They may not say exactly or as precisely what the historian meant to say, although this is rare. e.g. 'Combined with the NEP and the thaw in Russia's relations with other countries, this made some Bolsheviks fear the onset of a creeping reaction; they were haunted by fears of *Thermidor*'.

J. Roberts, *Europe 1880–1945* (London, 1972)

EXERCISE

Consider the following list of common historical words. What do they mean to you? Can you give them a *precise* definition? Compare them with a fellow student's definitions.

administration   movement   communications
trade   constitutional democratic
economic   reform   radical
political   class   authority
treaty   revolutionary power

Words like these occur constantly in historical writing. Consider the following example, which on the surface is simple to understand, but the precise meaning of which depends upon a careful scrutiny of key words.

'The cabinet **diplomacy** at which (Bismarck) excelled in the 1860s was no longer possible in the 1880s; **public opinion** was beginning to **influence** policy making it impossible to turn **friendships** on and off at will.'

W. Carr, *A History of Modern Germany* (London, 1969) p.185

What do you understand by such ordinary words? Is it precisely the same meaning that the historian meant to convey?

Be determined to define for yourself the exact meaning of words (like 'diplomacy'), especially when they are abstract (like 'influence'). *Do not let their meanings slip by, only vaguely perceived in your reading. Form mental pictures of what they are trying to say.* There will be cases, however, when the language is too abstract. The following sentence has a straight-forward meaning:

'on 15 July the government decided on war; on 19 July a formal declaration was delivered in Berlin and the Franco-Prussian war had begun'.

But can you fully understand the meaning of the following historical statements:

'The Ems telegram . . . was certainly designed to humiliate France and shift the advantage in the game of brinkmanship back to Berlin.'

'To conciliate the particularists, Bismarck agreed to extend the power of the Bundesrat,'

without (a) contextual knowledge (b) a precise grasp of the abstraction being used?

EXERCISE

Consider the following statement about the situation in Spain in 1930:

'. . . (it) was simultaneously a **moribund monarchy**, a country of very **uneven economic development**, and a **battleground** of ardent **political and intellectual cross-currents**'.

> G. Jackson, *The Spanish Republic and the Civil War, 1931–39* (Princeton, 1972) p.3

Try to form mental pictures of the words in bold type. Compare your understanding of these words with that of a fellow-student.

(i) What differences do you note?
(ii) What factors have produced this variation (e.g. your creative powers, your contextual knowledge, your understanding of vocabulary, etc.)?
(iii) How might you improve this capacity in the future?

It helps to rephrase words and terms. Metaphors, because they can often be unclear in their precise meaning, particularly should be paraphrased.

e.g. '(Stalin) ruthlessly swept aside opposition to collectivization and industrialization.'
'the (Russian) Revolution devoured its own makers.'
'(the split in the Liberal party) was the turning-point of British political history.'
'(Hitler) then used his mass support to castrate the forces which had resisted democracy.'

Re-state the above metaphorical statements in simpler language.

2. TECHNICAL LANGUAGE

Unlike books in some other subjects, such as physics or woodwork, history books do not have an extensive range of technical terms with precise, specialised meanings, (e.g. 'torque' or 'dovetail joint'). Such words do occur, however, in historical writings and you must familiarise yourself with them.

(a) *Contemporary Terms*

Certain terms frequently occur that would be commonly used in the modern period (e.g. 'rotten borough', 'Whig', 'disestablishment', 'tariff', 'bolshevism', 'pact').

SOME HINTS

Define these terms precisely and memorise them. Some textbooks include glossaries of such terms but a good dictionary is essential. To create an alphabetical listing on paper or cards can be a great help to you so that new terms can be entered as you come across them. Revise these terms periodically and often!

Be careful about contemporary words that seem familiar but may not have had the same meaning or implication in the modern period. (e.g. 'Tory', 'appeasement', 'dissenter', 'soviet', 'non-conformist'.)

Certain terms have an ambiguous or disputed meaning, sometimes provoking major historical discussion. (e.g. 'fascist', 'nationalism', 'class', 'imperialism'). If this is the case then you must be aware of it and carefully note the reasons for such differences of opinion.

(b) *Historical Labels*

Although historians examine evidence in minute detail, they are still forced to generalise about the past. They are interested in understanding the pattern of events and ideas; what things have in common as much as what makes them different.

e.g. to generalize about the significance of an event:
'The basic weakness of the Treaty (of Versailles) lay in the fact that it left the German people in a frame of mind not conducive to a lasting peace.

> G. Lichteim, *Europe in the Twentieth Century* (N.Y., 1972)

e.g. to generalize about people's motives:
'Gladstone's own particular crusade on Ireland was based on the concept of justice and fair dealing between nations . . .'
E. J. Feuchtwanger, *Gladstone*, (London, 1975)

As a result historians have developed a stock of general labels that are often used for convenience. Some, but not all of these were coined by contemporaries. They are very useful 'shorthand' descriptions and are only troublesome if you read or use them unthinkingly or as precise rather than generalised descriptions of the past; this they are not.

SOME HINTS

You must look beyond the generalisation to the particulars that these labels attempt to describe. You must be aware that such labels may not be appropriate for the whole of the period that you are studying.

Examples:

(i) Place Labels: e.g. Germany, Italy, Balkans, Hapsburg Empire, Middle-east.

(ii) Period Labels: e.g. The Age of Improvement, The Victorian Age, Weimar Germany, The Ancien Regime.

(iii) Event Labels: e.g. Cold War, blitzkrieg, nationalisation, appeasement, isolationism, The Great Depression.

(iv) People Labels: e.g. the bourgeoisie, working-class, the Great Powers, Central Powers, Slavs.

(v) Cultural and Movement Labels: e.g. civilization, laissez-faire, nationalism, neo-gothic, pan-Germanism, communism.

QUESTIONS

1. In the extract on p.20 consider the metaphors in lines 1, 4, 5–6 and 17–18.
   (a) What exactly do they mean?
   (b) Why has the historian chosen such language to make a historical point?
   (c) Can you re-phrase them to make the points clear?
   (d) Where else have metaphors been used.

2. Consider the collective nouns 'statesmen' (line 16) and ('Conservative and Liberal') 'governments' (line 46).
   (a) Who exactly does the historian mean?
   (b) What do these nouns imply about the number and type of people who supposedly adopted these attitudes?

3. Consider the following abstract nouns; 'influence' (line 1), 'tranquillity' (line 3), 'role' (line 14) and 'ally' (line 28).
   (a) What exactly do they mean to you?
   (b) How important are they to the historian's meaning?
   (c) Where else in the extract do such words innocently lurk?

4. The following labels are generalisations and may be challenged. How?
   'European' (lines 28 and 46), 'Continent' (line 30), 'pan-German' (line 34), 'Gladstonian Liberalism' (line 10).

5. (a) What technical terms can you find in the extract?
   (b) How have you defined them?

D. THE READING STRATEGY

There are four main stages in our reading strategy. Each of these has specific purposes, may require different reading speeds and demands a purposeful, critical attitude on your part.

A Summary of Stages, Speeds and Purposes

STAGE	GEAR/SPEED	PURPOSE
1. **Preview:** knowing what you want	—	1. To define your reading purpose. 2. To generate questions that you hope the book will answer.
2. **Overview:** discovering what you want	3/Skimming	1. To establish how relevant and useful the book is going to be. 2. To give you an idea about the structure of the book and how you might approach it. 3. To "trigger off" connections with your existing knowledge, making you more sensitive to the material at hand. 4. To give you an idea about: (a) the difficulty of the text (b) its scholarly stature.
3. **Inview:** understanding and selecting what you want	1/2/ Careful reading	1. To discover the main points, either (a) of the book or (b) for your reading task. 2. To separate the subordinate points. 3. To extract the relevant information.
4. **Review/ Recall:** assimilating what you have got	2/3	1. To confirm that (a) all the main points have been correctly identified and understood (b) your initial question-framework was valid and has been satisfied. 2. To encourage the filtering and re-ordering of information. 3. To reinforce recall of the main information.

The Purpose

The main purpose of your strategy is to provide a method of identifying and extracting relevant information efficiently. This whole process appears long-winded and complicated but once you are familiar with it you can employ the strategy very quickly. In the long-term it will save you time and effort.

SOME HINTS

Before you begin ensure that you have the following to hand:

1. Plenty of paper (scrap and good note-paper) for jotting down page numbers, quotations, thoughts provoked by your reading, full-scale notes at the end of the strategy.

2. Pencil and pen.

3. Dictionary for seeking out the meaning of every word you are uncertain about.

Ensure that your physical environment allows good levels of concentration. It is far easier in physical terms to read texts if they are positioned as below (A) rather than in the usual position (B). Try it!

A

B

(i) The Preview—knowing what you want

This is a crucial stage since it pre-determines what you want from a particular history book and therefore how you are to approach it.

A FRAMEWORK OF HISTORICAL QUESTIONS

The diagram below provides a crude outline of some of the main issues about which historians are concerned to ask questions and form judgements.

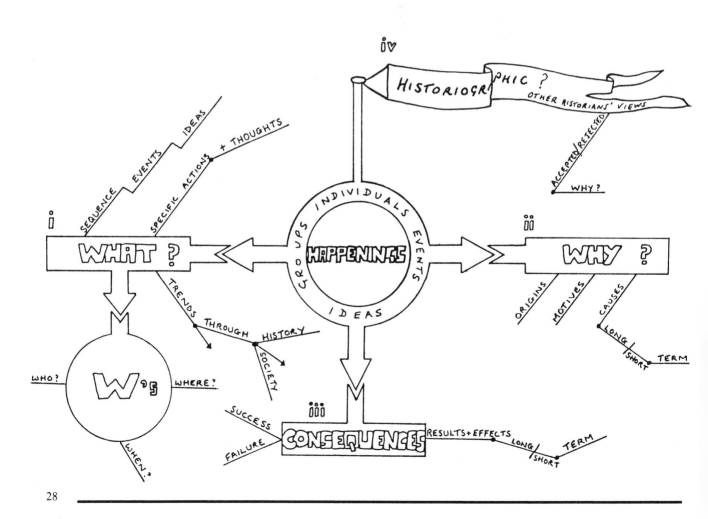

(ii) The Overview—discovering what you want

More than any other stage of our strategy, the Overview saves you time. It achieves this by being a quick survey and appraisal of the history book and by immediately establishing a perspective from which you can view the book.

It requires two skills:

(1) *A clear understanding of what you are looking for:*

(a) You must have a good framework of prior knowledge—of individuals, places, events, central ideas, etc.

(b) Look for keywords, often repeated, that indicate the whereabouts of your topic. Practice will improve this recognition.

(c) Learn to anticipate the main drift of the historian's treatment of the topic: Where are the main points to be found? How does the structure of the book (chapters, subsections, paragraphs) relate to your reading task?

(2) *Skimming and Sampling Techniques*

Read the pages very quickly. Whole chapters can be SKIMMED in minutes rather than hours. Use speedy, left-right movements of the eyes (perhaps 5–20 seconds per page). Using a finger or pen helps to guide the eye. Try it! You are looking for familiar words or phrases. If you recognise such words then explore the sentences around them. This SAMPLING is very important since it allows you to clarify points you have recognised and regain the drift of the historian's thoughts or arguments. Pay particular attention to the beginning and end of chapters, the first lines of paragraphs, and sub-headings and divisions in the book.

WHAT TO LOOK OUT FOR:

PUBLISHERS' BLURB

A concise understanding of the main subject of a book can be found on dust-covers and the backs of paper-bound books. Also be aware of other publications by an author, wherever listed.

TITLE PAGE

This will often tell you the general subject area (the title itself) and the level and kind of approach (the sub-title). T. O. Lloyd's *Empire to Welfare State* only helps your inquiries in the broadest sense. Compare this title with R. M. Stewart's *The Politics of Protection: Lord Derby and the Protectionist Party 1841–52.*

The author's *name and qualifications* should also be noted. This is not unimportant. Apart from acquiring factual information and an understanding of the author's main points of view, you should always be aware of the historiographical dimension. The more reading you do and the longer you study History, the more you will become alive to the quality and originality of what you are reading and the assumptions and values of the author. What qualifications does the author have? Is he familiar to you? Has your teacher made any comments about him? Where is he resident (school, college, university, freelance)?

On the back of the title page you will find reference to *the publishing history of the book*. History books are often considered to be out of date on the day of publication! This is an exaggeration, but you should remember that the older the history book (especially over 20 years) the less reliable it can be considered to be, because (i) new evidence is always being unearthed (ii) all historians tend to write from within the perspective of their own times ('every generation writes its own history') (iii) most professional historians update their own interpretations according to personal preference and in the face of scholarly criticism. All this does not mean that the more recent history books are necessarily the best. Try, however, to find the most up-to-date of an historian's works. A book published in 1960, reprinted in 1962, revised in 1968 and reprinted several times since only requires you to obtain a copy of the revised edition and not necessarily the most recent impression. Has it a long publishing history (many impressions)? How often have editions been revised (modified or updated)?

● TABLE OF CONTENTS

This is a very important page for telling you what is covered by the book and, if it is subdivided, how the topics are related to one another. It can greatly assist your understanding of the overall organisation of the book. Some contents-pages can be far from informative, however. Chapter titles like 'War', 'Post War', 'Pre War' and 'War' (from A. J. P. Taylor's *From Sarajevo to Potsdam*) do not help very much. The only alternative is to turn to the chapter itself and skim the pages for a clearer insight. If you are looking for a specific topic (e.g. The Paris Peace Conference) and it is not listed, you might investigate chapters which appear related (e.g. ''The Resettlement of Europe'' or, even more broadly, ''The First World War''). Also, consult the index whenever possible.

● INDEX

Most books (especially scholarly texts) contain an alphabetical listing of the occurrence of topics on specific pages. Indexes vary in quality and accuracy. Some are very brief and incomplete, while others provide an almost exhaustive break-down of main and subsidiary topics, cross-referencing subjects wherever necessary. Occasionally an author will provide separate indexes for people and events. The index is invaluable to the person who is merely seeking out information on a limited topic. An index can also help you establish whether the book is going to be of future use. Make a note of topics that the book usefully covers and keep it safe. Before you begin your closer reading of the text make sure that you consult the preliminary sections which follow the contents-pages but precede the main body of the book.

● PROLOGUES

Whether they be called Acknowledgements, Forewords, Prefaces or Introductions, these preambles can be very instructive for both the reader who is (still) uncertain about the usefulness of a history book and also the reader who is already committed to reading sections of it. The preambles will usually tell you:

(a) the main purpose and theses of the book.
(b) the way that the author intends going about proving his theses.
(c) (in a revised edition) the author's evaluation of scholarly criticism of early editions of the work and his counter-arguments.
(d) the range and quality of his collaborators (e.g. seminar discussions, research supervision, proof-readers, etc.).
(e) the type of student it is written for ('GCSE, 'A'-level, university, general reader).

By now you should have a fairly good idea of the possible use of a book. The page numbers of relevant sections should have been noted down together with the names of other potentially useful books and articles which the author has written.

● SKIM THE WHOLE BOOK

Even if you are certain in your mind about the usefulness/uselessness of a particular book, it is good practice to skim through the book from beginning to end. For the reader about to abandon the book this may easily uncover previously undisclosed information; for the committed reader it can add to his overall perspective on the book, thus helping him understand the relation of the parts to the whole, e.g. D. Marquand, *Ramsay MacDonald* (1977), is about more than a former Prime Minister. For both readers it might lead to topics (quotes, facts, ideas) of a wider interest than the task in hand (e.g. 'looking for information on 'Unemployment in the 1930s'). This skimming should be done very quickly (a few seconds per average page). Don't be concerned with the feeling that nothing is 'sinking in' but do try and seek out the main points. Often you will need to slow down to almost normal speed and sample sections.

Once you have become aware of the organisation of material in a particular book, the whole job of skimming becomes easier. Pay particular attention to the following if they are present:

(1) Section headings: (e.g. 'The Inter-War Years').
(2) Chapter headings: (e.g. 'The National Governments').
(3) Chapter sub-headings: (e.g. 'Post-War economies').
(4) Chapter 'flagging'—headings, marginalia, italics, bold type, etc. (e.g. 'mass unemployment').
(5) Chapter summaries—first and last paragraphs.
(6) Individual words and sentences—with practice the eye uncannily catches key words and phrases (e.g. 'almost 3 million in 1932' 'depressed areas', 'Jarrow March', '1934 Unemployment Insurance Act').

   This invaluable technique is greatly assisted by (a) prior knowledge of the topic (b) a clear definition of your reading purposes before tackling the book.
(7) The use of illustrations and diagrams.

(8) The inclusion and extensiveness of footnotes and bibliography. (What kinds of sources are mainly cited—primary and/or secondary? What kind of use is made of them—does he argue supplementary points in his footnotes?)

Your Overview of the book is now complete. It should have determined the relative usefulness of the text, suggested the best way of tackling it and provided you with an impression of the scholarly stature and historiographical viewpoint of the book.

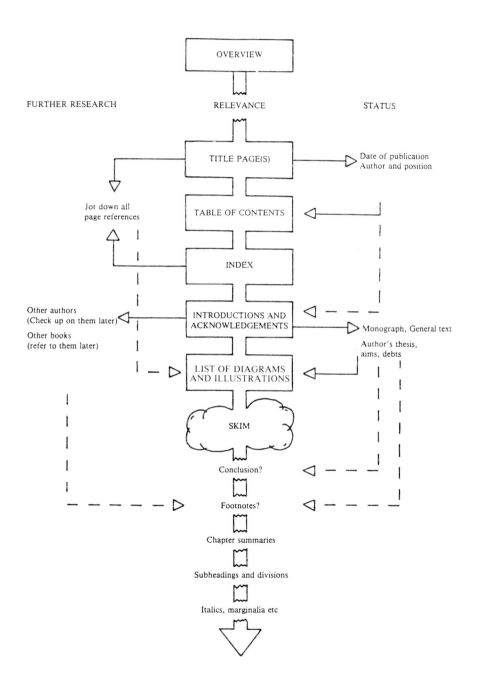

(iii) **The Inview—understanding and selecting what you want**

This stage of the strategy involves much more careful reading and analysis. You should begin with a rapid scan of the relevant section (already located by the Overview stage). Then you should read the section(s) carefully and critically, if necessary re-read the whole section. Finally, once you feel confident that you have selected the appropriate information, you can make notes and review your reading (see next stage of strategy). An efficient and effective Inview requires the following:

1. A very clear definition of what you want from the historian's text.

2. Flexibility in your reading speeds.

3. Always read actively, with a questioning attitude.

DISCOVERING THE MAIN POINTS— Where are they?

Analytical reading requires you constantly to separate the historian's main ideas from minor or subsidiary ones. This recognition of main points is at the heart of your task as a reader of history books and, later in the process, as a note-maker. Main ideas can be found at different levels in a book (see p.17).

1. *The main theses/themes of the work:* these will run through the whole book in varying forms and degrees. The book is essentially an attempt to substantiate these theses. The earliest expression of these ideas is in the historian's preambles

    e.g. 'The subject of this book is the transformation of European society since 1900 . . .'
    G. Lichtheim, *Europe in the Twentieth Century* (New York, 1972) xiii

2. *The chapter/section idea(s):* these will be much more concrete, are usually expressed in the first and/or last paragraphs and should be seen as a part of the wider themes/theses of the book.

    e.g. 'overall, the European system which collapsed into war in 1914 was highly unstable . . . When national passions were translated into imperialist politics, liberal-democratic institutions proved unable to keep the peace.' *ibid.* p.26

3. *The paragraph idea(s):* Most historians put just one main idea in each paragraph, often expressed in one sentence and usually placed at the beginning of the paragraph. The historian may well follow the same pattern throughout his book. Discover it!

    e.g. 'Nationalism was overwhelmingly the most important factor in European affairs . . .' *ibid.* p.25

Two problems arise at this stage of your strategy: distinguishing between main ideas and related, but subordinate, ideas and details; and knowing which of this secondary information to include in your notes. Both problems can be overcome with practice and an awareness of the technical difference between the two.

PROBLEM 1: Main Points

Two methods of resolving the first problem are:

(a) Identifying the main topic/noun in a paragraph/sentence (does it recur, in synonyms perhaps, later on? are there related or opposite words used?)

    e.g. 'The Liberal-Labour coalition, which had come into being around 1900, was committed to the extension of democracy.' *ibid.* p.23

The words 'vote', 'franchise', 'democracy' taken together, occur 10 times in one paragraph.

(b) Looking for clues:
    (i) Visual clues: italics, bold-type, numeration of points, etc.
    (ii) Verbal clues: historians often indicate that they are about to substantiate or qualify a main point through the use of particular words and phrases.

        e.g. 'firstly', 'on the other hand', 'for instance', 'furthermore', 'however', 'not always the case', 'therefore', 'equally'.

These verbal clues act as links between major and subordinate points.

Main ideas are also signalled.

e.g. 'fundamental', 'causes', 'led to', 'was the result of', 'significant', 'turning point', 'it is obvious that', 'indeed'.

WHICH ARE THE IMPORTANT DETAILS?

Having recognised the 'main point' in a chapter/paragraph you will not fail to notice that there are an awful lot of words left over! Historians do not make bald statements and always attempt to substantiate their point. This may take the form of supporting evidence, additional explanation or illustrative details and examples. Usually each main point has at least one important detail.

> e.g. 'As late as 1911 only 59% of Britain's adult male population (some eight million out of a total nearing forty-one million) had the vote, and there were seven different types of franchise, of which the two major ones related to ownership or occupation of land, or of any house defined as a separate dwelling.' *ibid.* p.23

PROBLEM 2: Details

The answer to 'how much detail should I include in my notes?' will depend upon the density of information in any given paragraph/section and your personal needs as a note-maker.

Generally you should include only:
(a) those subordinate ideas that are an integral part of the historian's argument.
(b) those details and examples that seem most successfully to illustrate the main points.

Remember that the historian's writings provide a personal analysis and are therefore trying to persuade the reader that the main ideas put forward are correct. Learn to see what follows on from the main ideas as a kind of proof.

EXERCISE

Consider again Evans' analysis of Palmerston and British diplomacy on p.20.

MAIN POINTS
1. What happened to British Foreign influence between 1815 and 1860?
2. Why were British statesmen preoccupied with Russia before 1860?
3. What suggestions are there in this extract that British influence in Europe was in decline during the middle decades of the nineteenth century?

DETAILS
4. What bolstered British influence abroad?
5. Why was Turkey a cause for concern?
6. Why did Britain miscalculate the Prussian threat?
7. What was Prussia's rise to prominence based upon?

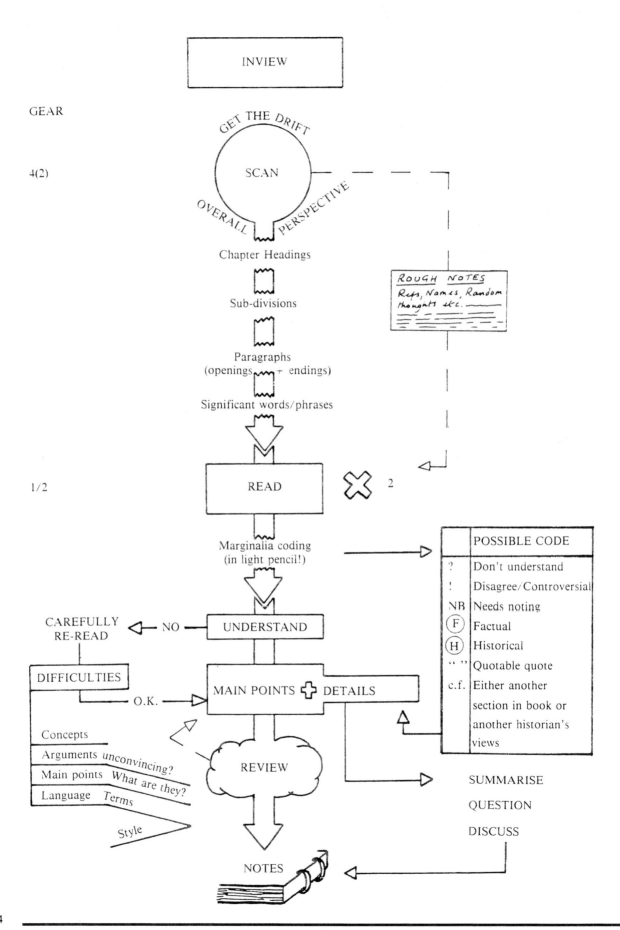

GEAR

4(2)

INVIEW

GET THE DRIFT

SCAN

OVERALL PERSPECTIVE

Chapter Headings

Sub-divisions

Paragraphs
(openings + endings)

Significant words/phrases

ROUGH NOTES
Refs, Names, Random
thoughts etc.

1/2

READ ✕ 2

Marginalia coding
(in light pencil!)

CAREFULLY
RE-READ ← NO ← UNDERSTAND

DIFFICULTIES

O.K. → MAIN POINTS ✛ DETAILS

Concepts
Arguments *unconvincing?*
Main points *What are they?*
Language *Terms*
Style

REVIEW

NOTES

	POSSIBLE CODE
?	Don't understand
!	Disagree/Controversial
NB	Needs noting
(F)	Factual
(H)	Historical
" "	Quotable quote
c.f.	Either another section in book or another historian's views

SUMMARISE

QUESTION

DISCUSS

(iv) Review and Recall

Review

The final stage of the strategy is *very important*. Obviously you cannot expect to understand everything at once. This applies to this book as much as to any other. You must practise recalling the main points—now and later.

(a) *It confirms whether you have correctly identified and understood the main points and separated them from the subsidiary details.*

> Quickly re-read the relevant sections and ensure that you haven't missed anything of importance.

> Check your original question-framework and make sure that (i) it was a valid one, (ii) you can answer the questions satisfactorily from the text, (iii) no new questions have arisen from your reading which affect your approach to the material.

(b) *It allows you to assimilate and summarise your main points/subsidiary detail in preparation for your notes.*

> This process of filtering and condensing is both practical and intellectually useful since it forces you to reduce the bulk of words and yet preserve the essential meaning of the text.

> Using *your own key words instead of the author's words* is difficult at first but will become easy with practice and will greatly assist later recall of information.

If your notes are to be the product of analytical thought, rather than a mere prelude to it, it is essential that you always review your reading.

Recall

Photographic memories apart, most people forget about 50% of what they've read within minutes of putting the book down, and 80% of it within twenty-four hours. More depressing still is the fact that a great proportion of that remembered 20% may not be the most important!

You will greatly assist both your *immediate understanding* of history texts and long-term recall of information if you *make a habit of trying to remember the main points*:

(i) during the Inview Stage (perhaps after a difficult paragraph and certainly every few pages).

(ii) after completing your Review (put your book and notes aside and go through the main points systematically until you know them thoroughly).

Recall is invaluable because:

(a) the knowledge that you will have to recall the main points will *keep you active*, sharpen your *concentration* and clarify the questions and headings you impose on the text.

(b) as the process is ongoing *your understanding of the author's line of argument* will not be interfered with but positively enhanced. You will be constantly interpreting and re-assimilating information, placing the parts of the argument in the (constantly developing) whole context of the author's thought.

DISCUSSION

In addition to the above methods of Review/Recall it will be found both enjoyable and informative if you cultivate the habit of discussing reading with friends and teachers. Discussion will bring the subject matter to life, and different viewpoints, both on the main points and the plausibility of the text, will be aired. This can be instructive and lively.

EXERCISE

While reading this chapter, have you been aware of the degree to which your reading method conforms to the advice offered here? It would be extremely useful for you to return to the whole chapter and apply the Strategy. This would help to ensure that you have mastered its main ideas on this crucial topic, and give you a first taste of the strategy in practice. Only a Review/Recall Stage at the end will determine how successful you have been in your reading.

A FINAL WORD

The chapter, and especially the Strategy, may seem to make the reading process far too time-consuming; a sledgehammer to crack an historical nut! Once mastered, however, it can be completed in minutes and ensure that you are reading at your optimum level.

E. CHECKLIST

1. Clearly distinguish between primary and secondary sources, and between the different types of history books.

2. Clarify your understanding of the main differences between narrative, description and analysis in historical writing.

3. Search for the different levels in books at which the historian presents his main ideas and arguments.

4. When beginning a new topic, consult general texts before you attempt more specialised or demanding reading.

5. When reading a new book, approach it from the *outside* (Title, introductions, index, skim reading, etc.) to the *inside* (main chapter and paragraph ideas etc.).

6. Take the necessary time to define clearly what kind of information you want from the book(s). Adjust your reading speed and method accordingly.

7. Approach historical texts in a questioning and active manner; consciously try to improve your level of concentration; develop your sensitivity to words and pictures in history books.

8. Take the necessary time to familiarise yourself with our reading Strategy (Preview—Overview—Inview—Review), so that you can employ it quickly and effectively.

9. If you are experiencing difficulties with your reading, are you able to pinpoint what is causing them?
   (i) difficult language and style
   (ii) slow reading speed
   (iii) low levels of concentration
   (iv) poor comprehension of ideas
   (v) inability to identify the main points (for your specific task) and separate these from secondary ideas, relevant supporting information, or superfluous material.

NOTE-MAKING

About this Chapter

The advanced study of History will primarily take the form of lectures, group discussions, individual reading and essay-writing. All these activities, to varying degrees, require students to make notes as a record for future reference. Students are constantly urged to 'make notes', and many respond with diligence. Fat files of notes are carefully cultivated throughout the course; only for students to find that the anticipated reward of examination success does not necessarily follow.

Inefficient and ineffective note-making methods often lie at the heart of students' inability to realise their potential. What follows is intended as a brief guide to the principles and practice of note-making. A number of different methods are discussed but:

(a) it is acknowledged from the outset that note-making, like many other aspects of studying, is essentially *a personal matter*. The student is encouraged to devise his own preferred note-making methods.

(b) it is hoped that some or all of the alternative methods here are used and combined by the student in his own system. *Different types of notes should be used for different learning purposes and different subject-matter.*

A. WHY BOTHER?

1. Notes provide the foundation on which all your other study activities can be based because:
   (a) your notes will allow you to get the most out of your individual reading and your lessons.
   (b) combined with reading and personal thought your notes will form the raw material of your essays.
   (c) your notes will eventually form the basis of your revision for examinations (internal and external) and will critically affect your chances of success.

2. Good note-making methods are invaluable to you as a student because:
   (a) they can positively assist learning and thus increase the possibility of greater historical understanding.
   (b) they are more efficient and thus save you time and work in the long term.

B. WHAT IS NOTE-MAKING ABOUT?

Note-making, fundamentally, requires you to understand the subject matter, select the relevant ideas and information and reorganise that material in a note-format. Whatever method you adopt, the following principles are equally valid and need to be taken into account.

1. Your notes should be the *product* of historical thought and not simply a *prelude* to it. This therefore implies a willingness on your part to:
   (a) reflect upon both the historical subject-matter and the form and content of your notes.
   (b) revise, alter and re-write your notes periodically in the light of increased understanding and information. This process of reflection and revision is crucial! It *is* difficult but will get easier with effort and practice.

2. Your notes are ultimately *a personal activity*. You must take time to devise a scheme that suits your own needs. The student with a very poor memory, for instance, may need to create more detailed notes than the student who retains facts easily.

3. Your notes should provide a *concise but comprehensive account* of a given topic. The exact amount of historical detail will again depend on individual needs. Resist the temptation to overburden your notes with too much information.

4. *Do not copy information unchanged.* Your understanding and ability to recall historical ideas and events will be better assisted by reformulating them into your own vocabulary and style. If a phrase is noteworthy then acknowledge the copying with speech marks and cite the source. Furthermore, strive to synthesise the various notes you make—from books, your own thoughts, television, etc. *Do not allow yourself to have several separate accounts of the same topic which duplicate one another.* You should regularly filter and funnel your information into a single set of notes. By doing so you will begin that vital process of critical analysis and revision at an early stage. The student who leaves the task of assimilation until examination time seriously undermines both his understanding of the subject matter, and of course, his chances of success in the examination.

5. Develop habits and techniques which make your notes *clear and interesting*. A visible structure needs to be given to your notes which reflects the analysis you have brought to the subject matter. Memorisation of material is also greatly helped by such a system. There follows a simple example of this kind of organisation of ideas and information. Alongside the notes are the kind of broad historical questions that you need to learn to ask about any topic and which have generated the headings.
   (a) HEADINGS AND SUB-DIVISIONS—are the most fundamental methods of structuring historical information. They require you to understand the subject matter and know what information you want to select from it. Headings immediately create an analysis, however crude or ill-informed, of historical information.
   (b) NUMBERING OF POINTS—can re-inforce the analytical structure by separating ideas and information, and, where appropriate, by creating a hierarchy of points. The advantages of such a system are that:

(i) it encourages both analysis and conciseness by forcing you to understand the similarities and differences between certain points.

(ii) it considerably helps memorisation of material (better, for instance, to have to remember that there were 5 key principles underlining the shape of the 1919 peace treaties rather than 'some' principles).

(c) SPACING AND INDENTING—can highlight both the separability of specific points/passages and also the relative importance of these to one another. As with the numbering system, a hierarchy of information can be suggested by indenting from the margins.

EXAMPLE

A student who is told to 'make notes on the diplomatic arrangement that followed the Napoleonic Wars' may use these simple techniques to create the following structure:

A Student's Preliminary
Question-Framework

Main Topic ——→	THE CONCERT OF EUROPE
Main Analytical Heading ——→	1. *THE NATURE OF THE 1815 SETTLEMENT*
Subordinate Heading ——→	(a) Purposes and Principles of Vienna.
	(b) The Main Terms.
	(c) Holy and Quadruple Alliances.
Special Issues ——→	(i) The Congresses
	(ii) The roles of Castlereagh and Canning
	(iii) The absence of consensus
	2. *METTERNICH AND CONSERVATISM*
	(a) Metternich's philosophy and Influence
	(b) Metternich's Domestic and Foreign Policies
	3. *THE FAILURE OF THE CONCERT*
	(a) The Achievements
	(b) Movements of Reform and Revolution (see other notes!) 1830–48
	(c) The Problems of Intervention

'What was the idea behind the Concert?'

'Were many alliances formed?'

'What was Metternich's role in all this?'

'Did the Concert succeed or fail?'

The student has identified and highlighted the three major aspects of the topic on which he is likely to be questioned. He has further sub-divided these into their key historical topics and, further still, identified the special issues that arise out of these topics.

(d) COLOUR, CAPITALS AND EMPHASES—provide more simple methods of enhancing clarity. Key words can be underlined in the same colour. Colour codes may be adopted to highlight information that belongs together. 'The Origins' of the English Civil War', could be noted with political factors written or shaded in blue, religious factors in red, economic in green, and so forth. The ability to visualise areas on the page is an important revision technique and would be greatly helped by such codes.

(e) ABBREVIATIONS—usually form a part of every student's notes. Developing your own system can be fun and challenging. At the very least it would greatly increase the speed at which you took notes and also reduce a little of the bulk of your burgeoning files! Latin abbreviations, algebraic symbols, contractions of words and personal inventions can all be used. Whatever abbreviations you use, however, apply them consistently and often. The more you use them, the more easily they will come to you and the more personal and particular will their meaning be.

Some Common (and not so Common) Abbreviations	Definitions
ap.	in the writings of
c.	century, chapter, or about
Cf.	compare with
et al.	and others, and elsewhere
ff.	following
→	leads to, towards
∵	because
∴	therefore
≠	is not equal to
⇔	equivalent to
~	difference

EXAMPLE

'Palmerston's three periods of foreign policy strengthened Britain's influence in Europe, although his bullying methods led to anger among Britain's wartime allies. This success before 1841 does not compare with the periods following 1846 and 1855, mainly because of the differences in the international scene after that time.'

'P.'s 3 periods of for. pol. strengthened B.'s influence in Epe.—but bullying methods → anger (B.'s wartime allies). Success before 1841 > after 1846 + 1855 ∴ ~'s in international scene.

EXERCISE

THE EASTERN QUESTION

Below are two examples of a student's notes. The first was taken during a lesson. The second was taken at a later date, using a single source (D. Thomson, *Europe Since Napoleon*, 1977) for its information.

1. Consider each one separately and try to apply the guidelines and hints that have been offered so far. What criticisms would you make of both notes with regard to their:
   (a) content?
   (b) presentation?
   (c) organisation?

2. Progress in note-making requires an honest appraisal of your own notes. How closely do they resemble these notes?

   Make a list of deficiencies that could be remedied by you.

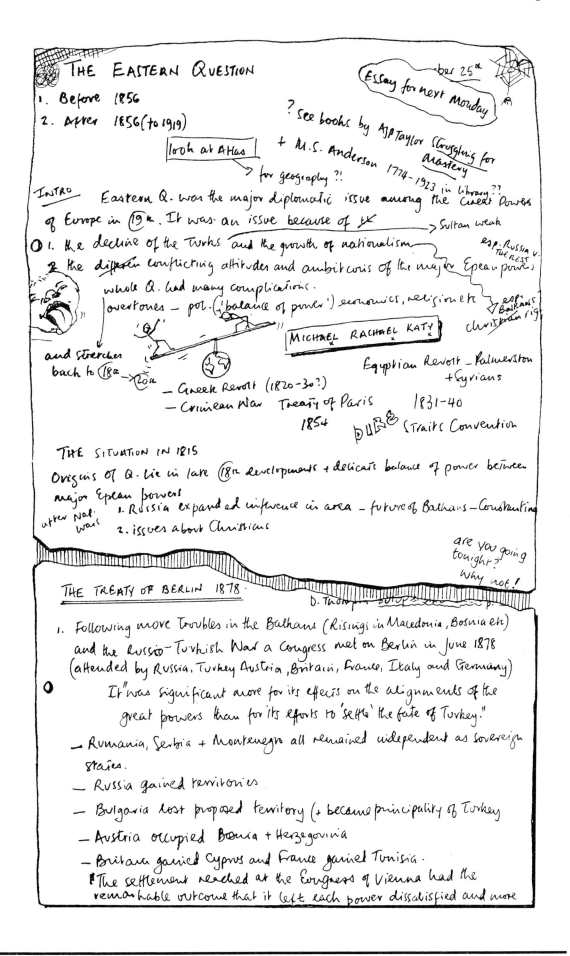

THE EASTERN QUESTION

1. Before 1856
2. After 1856 (to 1919)

Essay for next Monday -ber 25th

look at Atlas

? See books by AJP Taylor Struggling for Mastery
+ M.S. Anderson 1774-1923 in library ??
→ for geography ?!

INTRO Eastern Q. was the major diplomatic issue among the Great Powers of Europe in 19th. It was an issue because of it ── → Sultan weak
O 1. the decline of the Turks and the growth of nationalism ──
2. the different conflicting attitudes and ambitions of the major Epean powers
esp. Russia v. THE REST
whole Q. had many complications.
overtones ── pol. ('balance of power') economics, religion etc → esp. Balkans Christian rig
christian rig

and stretches back to 18th → 20th

MICHAEL   RACHAEL   KATY

── Greek Revolt (1820-30?)
── Crimean War   Treaty of Paris 1854   pure Straits Convention

Egyptian Revolt ── Palmerston + Syrians
1831-40

THE SITUATION IN 1815

Origins of Q. lie in late 18th developments + delicate balance of power between major Epean powers
after Nap. wars
1. Russia expanded influence in area ── future of Balkans ── Constantin
2. issues about Christians

are you going tonight? Why not !

THE TREATY OF BERLIN 1878.

D. Thomp... Euro...

1. Following more troubles in the Balkans (Risings in Macedonia, Bosnia etc) and the Russo-Turkish War a Congress met on Berlin in June 1878 (attended by Russia, Turkey Austria, Britain, France, Italy and Germany)
O   It "was significant more for its effects on the alignments of the great powers than for its efforts to 'settle' the fate of Turkey."
── Rumania, Serbia + Montenegro all remained independent as sovereign states.
── Russia gained territories
── Bulgaria lost proposed territory (+ became principality of Turkey
── Austria occupied Bosnia + Herzegovina
── Britain gained Cyprus and France gained Tunisia.
* The settlement reached at the Congress of Vienna had the remarkable outcome that it left each power dissatisfied and more

C. WHAT DO I NEED NOTES ON?

The problem of deciding what is relevant and important is at the centre of your task as a note-maker. Even when you have solved this difficult problem there is the further question of quantity; 'how much should I write?'

1. THE NARRATIVE—purely descriptive notes have little place in your advanced study of History. Your major concern lies with under-standing and analysing this body of infor-mation—the 'why' and 'how' of History, rather than the 'what'. Your notes should, as concisely as possible, indicate the story 'what happened', 'when' and 'with whom'. Where the sequence of information is important to the understanding of a given topic (for instance, the origins of the Unification of Italy or the setting up of the National Governments, 1931–39) you must develop a system that clearly but succinctly shows the connections between events and ideas and also pinpoints continuities/discon-tinuities in a line of development.

2. THE ANALYSIS—the precise way in which you dissect an historical topic will largely deter-mine which information is relevant and needs to be noted. The advanced study of History demands far more than a retentive memory for facts or an ability to describe fluently the course of an historical event. The questions on p.47 demand to know 'why' and 'how'. They inquire into the *consequences* of historical events. They are intrigued by the *connections* between dif-ferent people, ideas and events. You must:

   ask yourself these questions.
   apply them to your source of information.
   ensure your note-structure reflects these questions.
   gather sufficient information in your notes to be able to answer these questions.

Furthermore, your analysis must take account of any historiographical dimension. In other words, you must accept the idea that historians often disagree and may have convincing reasons to support their individual viewpoints. Your notes should record these differences.

Generally speaking, the answer to our question '*What do I need notes on?*' depends upon two considerations:

YOUR TASK: often you will have been given an explicit purpose for making notes at the outset.

e.g. At the beginning of a lesson you may be told that you are to 'make written notes on the rise of Louis Napoleon, paying particular atten-tion to his sense of historic mission, his coups and his writings'.

You may be asked to 'begin note-making and reading for an essay/class discussion on the reasons for Labour's 1945 election victory'.

In both cases you have been given an explicit and specific purpose and *your notes should be deter-mined by this task.*

YOUR SUBJECT-MATTER: in the absence of a clear directive about what you need from given information, your first task is to decide which questions are appropriate to the information being presented to you (by a teacher or a book).

The answer to our second question '*How much do I need to write?*' will be affected significantly by:

(a) your note-making system and formats (see later discussion on pp.49 and 62).
(b) your strengths and weaknesses as a student (genius? well-read in period? lousy memory? big handwriting!).
(c) your note-making task.
   Essays, class reports, etc. will tend to be very narrow in focus and deal only with one aspect or issue. Notes for this purpose are usually selective and may be discarded (either after use or once integrated into your permanent notes). Finished notes on major topics and questions need to include:
   (i) main analytical points and ideas.
   (ii) secondary ideas which develop, qualify or prove (i).
   (iii) at least one factual example to illustrate (i) and (ii).

YOUR NARRATIVE
THE DESCRIPTION

⬇

WHAT & WHEN

1. What are the main events/characteristics/ideas that constitute a period/movement/idea/event in the past?

2. When did such things happen?

3. Is there an important or obvious *sequence* to these events?

4. Do *parallels* exist in other places or time-periods?

WHO

1. Who are the main individuals involved in an event? What do you know of them?

2. Is it possible to determine who are the most influential individuals in terms of either their ideas or actions?

TERMINOLOGY

1. What is the meaning of technical/specialised terms?

2. Does historical debate centre itself upon the meaning of certain terms?

CAUSES

MOTIVES

RESULTS

1. Was the event/idea/method a success or failure?

2. How influential was an idea on future developments?

3. What were the consequences of an event in the short or long term?

ORIGINS

CHANGE/CONTINUITY

5. Is it possible to pin-point turning-points in the past when
   (a) one period becomes significantly different from another ('periodisation') or
   (b) decisions are made by individuals which significantly affect the outcome of some future event?

YOUR ANALYSIS
THE EXPLANATION

⬇

WHY

1. What background circumstances made an event or idea (a) possible (b) probable?

2. What factors (people, events and ideas) long before an event occurred ('preconditions') were necessary before it could take place?

3. What factors present immediately before an event can be said to have directly provoked it?

4. Of all these factors (1, 2 and 3 above) is it possible to select the most important cause(s) of an event or idea in the long or short term?

5. What were the personal motives of the chief participants in an event?

6. How varied/uniform were these motives?

7. How much are the individuals responsible for events and how much are they caused by 'external' factors:
   (a) other people and ideas?
   (b) local and national developments (e.g. economic distress, political changes, religious reforms, etc.)?
   (c) chance?

HOW

1. What is the starting-point of a person's career, an idea or movement?

2. What are the long-term developments that contribute to an event rather than cause it?

3. To what extent have ideas, movements and institutions changed over a period of time (a) in form (b) in substance?

4. What elements of continuity remain during movements of apparent change?

TAKING NOTES

SOURCE OF INFORMATION	SOME HINTS
LESSONS/LECTURES	1. Determine your *teacher's style* and method: (a) how does he emphasise key points → ↗ voice changes? → on board? ↘ by dictation? (b) when does he emphasise key points → ↗ end of lesson? → at intervals? ↘ never? 2. Look and listen for *the central ideas*. You want an *overall structure to a topic* as well as specific information. Do not be tempted to record every syllable. Once you have the 'shape' of the topic you can add detail and shading later. 3. Develop a *regular system* for lesson notes: (a) it will speed up note-making. (b) it frees you to respond to information in an analytical way. 4. Be aware of *recommended reading* and page references. 5. Do not think of lesson notes as finished products; they are rough, *interim reports*. 6. Lessons last until the teacher ends them. Stay awake! *Concentrate until the very end*, since key ideas and themes may be summarised at this point.

AUDIO-VISUAL
(taped discussions, T.V. programmes, slides, etc.)
	1. Decide whether this source is meant to:
	(a) be the major input of information or
	(b) supplement and complement an existing knowledge.
	
	If (a) then points 1 to 5 above apply.
	If (b) then select only those points (ideas, facts, differing interpretations) that substantiate and clarify your existing knowledge.
	Integrate these points into your main notes later.
	
	2. Note the different types of historical evidence that are often (incidently, perhaps) depicted in slides and T.V. programmes.

BOOKS, PERIODICALS	1. Familiarise yourself with the Strategy on p.27 and learn to be *purposeful, active and flexible* in your reading habits. 2. *Make rough notes on separate sheets* (key ideas, page references, names of other books to consult) as you go along (usually after skimming the text p.29). 3. Do not attempt to create a neat copy in you note-making immediately. Notes following reading or lessons, must be *reviewed, supplemented and re-organised*. 4. (a) Use the historian's *key topic-points*, in a paraphrased form, as the basis of your own notes. (b) Add subordinate ideas only if they are an *integral part* of the historian's argument. (c) Add examples and supporting factual detail only insofar as they successfully *illustrate and substantiate the main points*.

D. SOME ALTERNATIVE NOTE-MAKING METHODS

There are different ways of making notes, all of which have their individual strengths and weaknesses. You should try to develop different methods for different kinds of historical information. Both the actual process of creating such notes and the appropriateness and variety of the finished product will aid understanding and memorisation.

Card Indexes

The most convenient method of keeping a note of important individuals and terminology is a card file or index. Significant information about people and definitions of unfamiliar or important terms, can be quickly recorded on a small card (usually 13cms x 8cms is adequate) and then filed alphabetically in a box, marked either 'BIOGRAPHICAL INDEX' or 'GLOSSARY'. Cards and boxes can either be bought from a stationer or made out of ordinary file paper and shoe boxes! Marker cards which indicate either names (e.g. 'IMPERIALISM' or 'R. PEEL') or letters (i.e. 'A', 'B', 'C' etc.) should be inserted at appropriate places to allow for quick reference. Cards are also a useful device for revision. A periodic perusal of your cards will quickly ensure a sound (and relatively painless!) knowledge of important people and terms.

A typical entry in the glossary may be as follows:

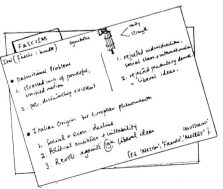

It could be filed under 'Fascism' or, simply, 'F'.

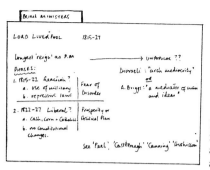

Relevant information can be added to the cards as the need arises.

Linear Notes

By far the most common method of note-making involves the arrangement of information and ideas in a linear form (my notes here, for instance!). Too often this is the only form of note in a student's file.

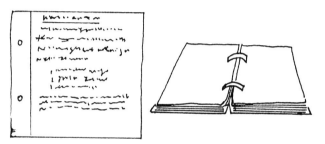

Linear notes are too often made by history students for the wrong reasons:
(a) they are familiar to the student and relatively easy to write.
(b) they appear to be 'neat'.
Both these reasons, however, may work against your adoption of a more effective and efficient approach to note-making.

THE DISADVANTAGES OF LINEAR NOTES

1. They can encourage a mindless transcription of information from textbook to note-page. You may fill a file with such notes and yet not understand a thing!

2. They tend to be finite. It is difficult, and often appears unnecessary, to add information to such notes. Apart from the obvious question of space (where on earth do you put the new material—in the margin? in between the lines? on a separate sheet? rewrite the whole page? how many times?!) there is the more serious problem that linear notes can give the impression of being comprehensive and exhaustive. That will rarely be the case! They also make it

difficult to show connections and relationships between different information on the same page or elsewhere in your file.

3. There is strong evidence to suggest that the brain does not cope with information in a simple, linear form. It prefers ideas to be presented in a more complex, multi-dimensional manner. There should be room in your note-file, therefore, for charts, diagrams and pattern-notes as well as the more conventional linear format.

Advanced level History does demand very detailed knowledge and for this purpose the linear note is very appropriate.

SOME HINTS

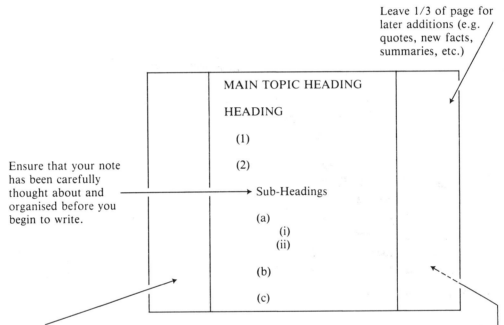

Leave 1/3 of page for later additions (e.g. quotes, new facts, summaries, etc.)

MAIN TOPIC HEADING

HEADING

(1)

(2)

Ensure that your note has been carefully thought about and organised before you begin to write.

Sub-Headings

(a)
   (i)
   (ii)

(b)

(c)

Natural margin can be used to pencil-in queries and uncertainties in your understanding. Do not let such things slip by.

Only write on one side. The reverse side can be used for supplementary notes and information at a later date. It also allows you to cut-up your notes for the purpose of later re-organisation.

EXERCISE

Return to the extract on p.2 ('The New Europe'). Following our general advice on making notes and the specific suggestions above, try to make a detailed note about the fundamental changes in European society.

Pattern Notes

If you are to fulfil the examiner's expectations you must learn to use historical information in an *analytical and flexible way*. At the very least your notes should not discourage you in this aim. At

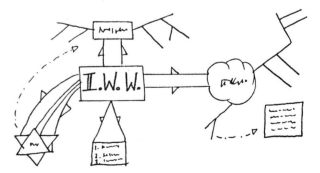

their best your notes can stimulate historical analysis, clarity of thought, and personal interest. Pattern-notes (sometimes called 'mind-maps') can fulfil many of your basic requirements of analytical note-making and they have a number of advantages over their over-used linear equivalent.

PRINCIPLES OF MAKING PATTERN NOTES
(© Buzan, *Use your Head* (B.B.C. London 1974).)

1. You begin at the centre or main idea (rather than at the top) and branch out as dictated by the individual ideas and general form of the central theme. The centre or main idea is therefore more clearly defined.

2. The relative importance of each idea is clearly indicated. More important ideas will be nearer the centre and less important ideas will be near the edge.

3. The links between the key concepts will be immediately recognised because of their proximity and connection.

4. As a result of the above, recall and review will be more effective and rapid.

5. The nature of the structure allows for the early addition of new information without messy scratching out or squeezing in etc.

6. Each pattern will be different from each other pattern. This will aid recall.

7. In the more creative areas of note-making such as essay preparations etc. the open-ended nature of the pattern will enable the brain to make new connections far more readily.

Or, to put this all differently . . .

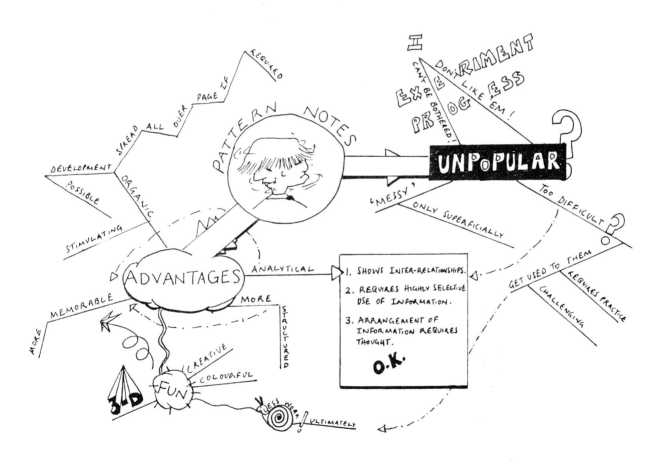

Pattern-notes arrange information spatially to create memorable and coherent patterns. They rely both upon colour and a variety of simple visual devices. The creative element in such notes is limited only by the imagination of you, the user.

KEY-RECALL WORDS:
DISCOVERING AND INVENTING THEM

History is a wordy subject. Your notes, however, should strive to be concise and need to be stripped of unnecessary words. Learning to identify key ideas is therefore one of your most important and difficult tasks as a student of History.

Pattern note-making requires you to:

(a) discover the historian's key ideas and his most significant supporting details.

(b) transform this information into a series of single words that simplify and summarise the historian's argument, without also distorting it beyond recognition and recall. The key-words you adopt for your pattern-note must easily recall a specific meaning for you.

e.g. '. . . the French never had any intention of opposing the German reoccupation of the Rhineland. The French military authorities held that, since their army was incapable of invading even the demilitarised Rhineland, the reoccupation would make no real difference. The French politicians were only concerned to exploit the affair by extracting a promise of future support from the British.'

A. J. P. Taylor,
English History, 1914-45.
(Oxford 1965), p.387.

might become . . .

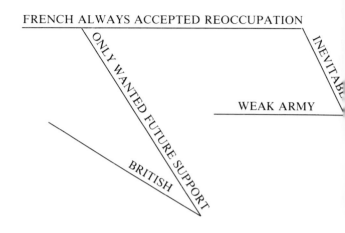

. . . 12 words as against 58!

EXERCISE: CONSTRUCTING A PATTERN-NOTE

EUROPE'S RULING CLASS

Stage One: Discovering the key words.

Read the extract on p.16 concerning the ruling class.

(a) Try to identify the main points and supporting details.

(b) Then identify (and write on paper) the key-words that the historian uses. These are the basis of your pattern-note.

After you have done this, compare your key-words with the list below. Discuss the reasons for those chosen.

| 'monarchy' | 'prevalent form of government' |

| 'only two republics' | 'apex of society' |

'the most important persons on the European political stage'

'to tie European society together'

| 'leaders of society' | '. . . seemed an anomaly' |

'reinforced a traditional hierarchy'

'guaranteeing . . . an established order'

'alliance . . . with the army and the landed aristocracy'

'industry and commerce became dominating factors'

'agriculture still . . . important'

SOME HINTS

1. Be succinct.

2. Select your own key-words carefully. They must faithfully convey the historian's meaning and still be memorable for you.

3. Arrange your information in pencil to allow for amendments.

4. Learn to paraphrase the historian's argument (a) as you are reading (b) after selecting his key words.

Stage 2. Transforming the Information

This requires you to understand the historian's main argument, be able to separate main points from supporting detail and substitute your own key-words for the historian's vocabulary.

e.g. The passage on p.16 argues that *monarchy* provided *the important political people* in Europe because of its *universality* as a *form of government* and because it *embodied the values and aspirations* of contemporary society—monarchy *led society* (e.g. patronage) and also fulfilled *conservative role* by *sanctioning the established order*—monarchy's authority and status in large part derived from *alliance* with the *landed aristocracy* and *army*—the *rise* of industrial and commercial classes *challenged* this *status quo* as the *new providers of national wealth*, though *agriculture still important*—industrialists *absorbed* into status quo.

EXERCISE: COMPARING LINEAR AND PATTERN NOTES

THE NATIONAL REVOLUTIONS, 1848-50.

Read D. Thomson, *Europe Since Napoleon* (London: 1966), pp.204-234. Make your usual linear notes. Then compare your results (one two, three—more?! pages) with the pattern-note on the same topic. Ask the following questions of your notes:

Do they demonstrate the main point of Thomson's discussion (i.e. the diverse but interconnected nature of the revolution)?

Do they provide a clear overview of the topic, especially the causes and consequences?

Do they exclude some information either because it is inappropriate here (e.g. the sequence) or excessively detailed (e.g. the scale of the reaction in 1850)?

Furthermore, have you noted in a different place:

(a)　(i) Metternich's System.
　　 (ii) 'Nationalism' 'Liberalism' and 'Socialism'
　　 (iii) the Hapsburg Empire
　　 (iv) industrial change and social distress

(b) individuals who seem important?
　　 (i) Guiseppe Mazzini
　　 (ii) Louis Philippe
　　 (iii) Kossuth
　　 (iv) Lamartine

(c) unfamiliar terminology?
　　 (i) feudalism
　　 (ii) free trade
　　 (iii) Bund, Diet and Reichstag
　　 (iv) absolutism
　　 (v) Risorgimento
　　 (vi) Robot

No? Why Not?!

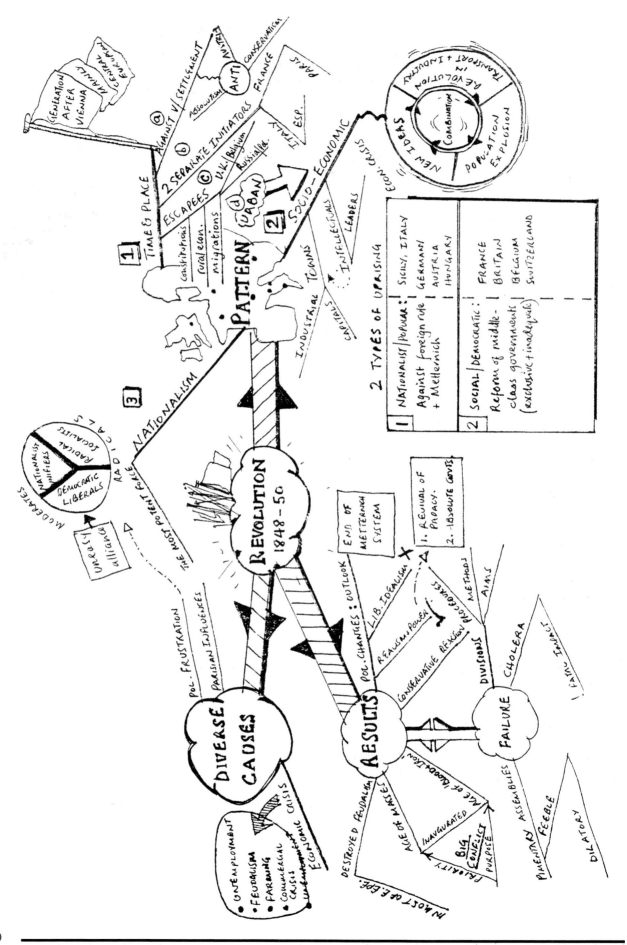

Diagrams and Tables

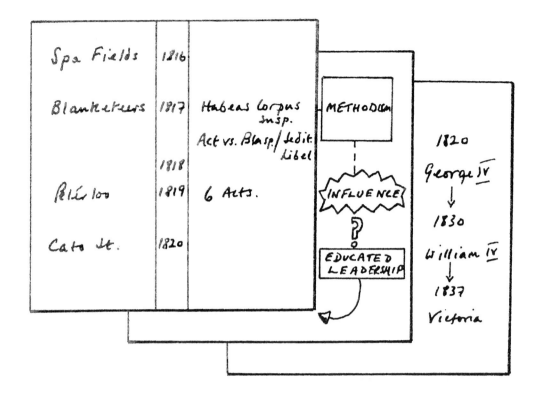

Reorganising information in diagrammatic form has strong advantages and disadvantages. Your decision as to whether a diagram is appropriate largely depends upon the purpose of the note and the quantity of information that is needed (see below).

The Advantages:

1. They clearly show the relationship between facts and encourage the note-maker to be more analytical and selective in his approach to historical information. Use them not only to record information, but also to explore your understanding of historical topics and issues.

2. Diagrams have a strong visual impact. This stimulates the note-maker's imagination and also tends to make the note memorable.

The Disadvantages of Diagrammatic Notes

1. They cannot carry great quantities of information.

2. They simplify, and may therefore distort, historical questions. Where connecting lines are used, they do not indicate the full nature or complexity of the connection. (e.g. the precise extent of a Prime Minister's influence over his cabinet or the minor events that occur between two noted happenings.)

EXAMPLES

1. *To show the sequence of ideas or events.*

Accounts of simple narrative can be shown in the form of time-lines. Used in a limited way they are very effective. Narrow topics like 'Whig reforms 1830–41' or 'the suffragette movement' are less likely to be overburdened with detail than more general topics like 'British foreign policy, 1815–65' or 'Britain's inter-war economy'.

Time-lines can be used to describe a chronological narrative of events or to help you to analyse the inter-relationships' of different factors, events and places. Gaining an overall perspective is an important task when encountering a new topic. Compare the two treatments of related but separate topics.

ORIGINS OF 1914-18 WAR

	ARMS RACE	ALLIANCE SYSTEM	COLONIAL CONFLICT
1890		• Franco-Russian Entente.	• Dismissal of Bismarck.
		• Franco-Russian Alliance.	
1895			
	• German 1st Navy Law / Navy League formed.		• Fashoda Crisis (Br. + Fr.).
	• German 2nd Navy Law.		• Start of Boer War.
1900		• Anglo-Japanese Alliance: end of 'splendid isolation'.	• Russo-Japanese war.
		• French-British Entente.	• Dogger Bank incident.
1905	• British 'Dreadnought' built.	• Russo-German Treaty.	• 1st Morroccan Crisis.
	• German 3rd Navy Law.	• Algerias Conference.	
	• Failure of Hague Arms Conf.		• D.Telegraph interview - Kaiser.
	• German 4th Navy Law.	• Anglo-Russian Entente.	• A-Hung. annexe Bosnia.
	• British Navy Law.		
1910			• 2nd Morroccan Crisis
	• Failure of Haldane Mission.		• Tripoli War (It. + Turkey)
	• Brit. and Germ. Army / Navy		• 1st Balkan Wars

QUESTIONS

Study the incomplete diagram that represents 'The Decline of the French Monarchy'.

(a) Use the information provided to complete the blank areas.

(b) Assess the merits of this particular diagram. Does it help you to analyse the information? Has it made the ideas more memorable?

What do you feel are the most important deficiencies of these notes and how might you remedy them?

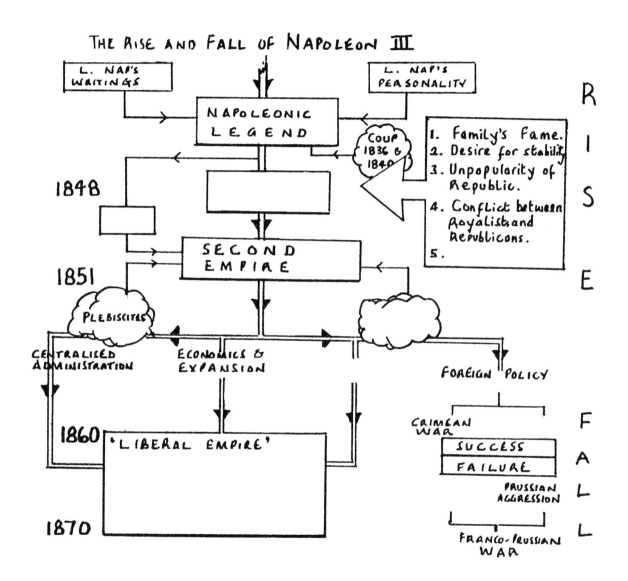

THE RISE AND FALL OF NAPOLEON III

1800 CONSTITUTION.

COUP 2 DEC.

PRESIDENT OF FRENCH REPUBLIC.

Publicity about 'Social question'.

STATE CLOSE TO CHURCH.

ITALIAN POLICY

MEXICAN EXPEDITION

2. *To show connections between historical information*

Historical events are often complicated, especially if you try to explain why they happened (the causes), or how they were possible (the origins), or what the results were (the effects). These events are complex because often more than one factor or person is involved, humans do not always reveal their true motives and the historical evidence may be inadequate. Nonetheless, understanding what caused things to happen (causation) and why individuals acted in particular ways (motives) is one of your most fundamental tasks. Diagrams can help you to record such questions in a clear and interesting way. They also encourage you to explore and rearrange the different components of an event to develop your understanding.

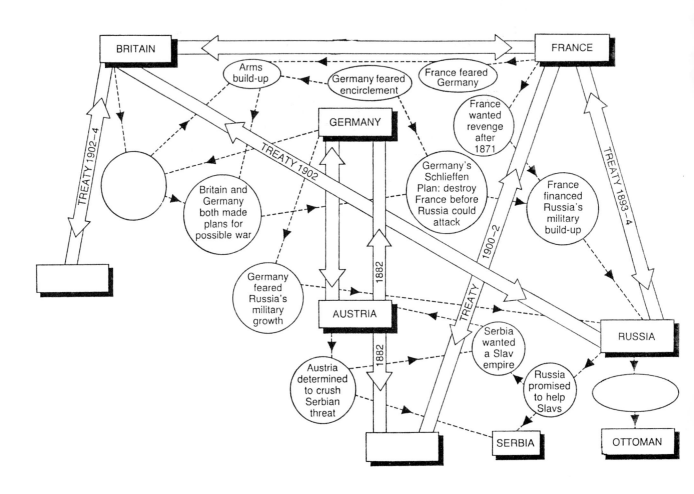

THE TANGLED WEB OF
EUROPEAN DIPLOMACY
c.1914.

TREATY—1904	Serbia wanted a Slav Empire.
TREATY—1879	
ITALY	Rivalry over empires and navies.
JAPAN	

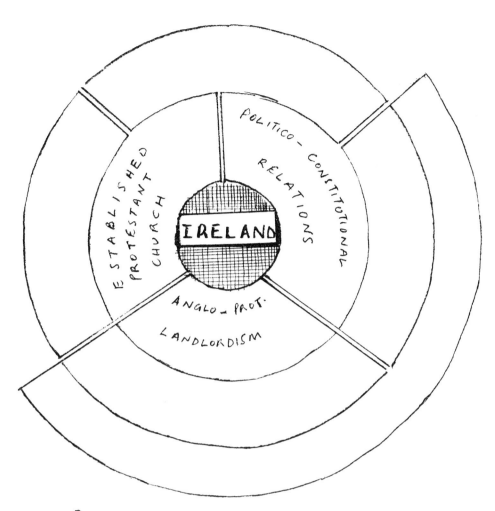

" [Gladstone] had his own causes, principally Ireland, which he pursued, sometimes beyond the limits of practical politics."

E. J. Feuchtwanger. *Gladstone*. p. 230

Coercion Acts (1870/81/82)

University Bills (1870)

Land Acts (1870/81)

Home Rule Bills (1886, 1893)

Church Bill (1869)

(a) These diagrams are partially completed. Use the information to complete each one fully.

(b) Discuss the merits and demerits of using this form of note to reveal the ways historical information can inter-connect (e.g. the direction of the relationship).

More abstract diagrams ranging from the simple to the complex, can be invented by you to show historical sequences, such as the development of an idea or movement (e.g. liberalism) or the general changes and continuities that may occur within that idea.

3. *To show similarity and difference in historical information.*

Historical understanding (at least in the early stages of exploring a topic) often depends upon your ability to recognise the ways in which people, ideas or events are similar and different. This may apply to a particular period or it may be concerned with changes over a long period of time.

Charts (or tables) are the simplest way to record this kind of information by categorising people, ideas and events.

e.g:

APPEASEMENT
THE MOTIVES OF BRITISH FOREIGN POLICY IN THE 1930s

Year	SYMPATHY FOR GERMANY (VERSAILLES)	SELF-DEFENCE (HOME/EMPIRE)	GERMAN AGGRESSION (ANXIETY ABOUT)	PRACTICALITY (STRATEGY + FINANCE)	MAIN INFLUENTIAL FACTORS
1931	Lenience over reparations. Non-support after French reoccupation of Ruhr.	Statute of Westminster		growing independence of Dominions	• Econ. Consequences of the Peace (Keynes). W • 'Anti-War literature'. A
1932		Ten Year rule dropped		Ten Year Rule 2nd Disarmament Conference.	• Oxford Union Debate. R • E. Fulham by-election. R
1933					
1934		Hoare-Laval Pact. Non-support of French intervention in E.Ups + Spain.	Hoare Pledge: Collective security. Stresa Front.	Hoare-Laval Pact	• League of Nations Union P + "Peace Ballot". H
1935	Non-reaction to Saar reoccupation. Anglo-German naval Treaty.	• Defence White Paper: airforce priority.		Defence White Paper: air force priority Non-intervention in Sp.	• Concept of "Limited Liability" + opposition to "continental" commitment. O B • Concern about Japanese threat in Far East. A
1936	Non-reaction following Rhineland reoccupation.	• Rearmament programme begins.			• Outbreak of Spanish Civil War. A
1937		• Chamberlain dialogue with dictators	Munich Conference.		• Major rearmament in Germany.
1938				Britain recognised Franco regime in Sp.	• U.S. Neutrality Acts/isolation. • Distrust of Russia. O
1939		Declaration of War against Germany.	Guarantee to Poland; Greece + Rumania. Anglo-Turkish Pact.		• Invasion of Church + change in public opinion. O • Nazi-Russia Pact. O • invasion of Poland
1940					

Spider notes

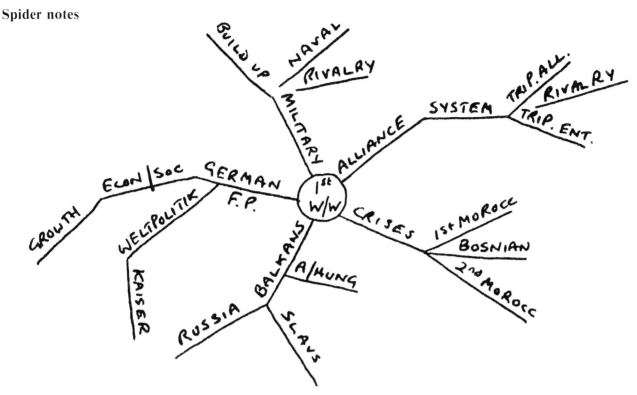

Yet another method of making notes involves you in a 'brain storming' exercise in which you allow your memory to recall any information you can associate with a particular topic or question. It may strike you as unusual but, once mastered, it can be used very quickly and effectively for a variety of purposes:

    (a) Essay planning

    (b) Revision exercises

    (c) General clarification of your thoughts on specific topics and questions (for a single student or a group of individuals)

METHOD

1. Take a central idea (e.g. 'Stalinist Russia'). Place this idea at the centre of a large blank sheet of paper.

2. Using all the words that come to you spontaneously and in sequence 'spray' your information (names, facts, concepts), however irrelevant or bizarre, along lines that run outwards from your central idea.

3. Do not censor this flow of information or consciously reflect upon it. If your flow of ideas dries up, return to your central idea and wait for a new thought.

    This note-making activity can be very speedy and frenetic—indeed, it should be if the ideas are arriving spontaneously.

4. Carefully survey the bizarre pattern in front of you, once your thoughts have been exhausted. Consider each individual word and sequence.

    (a) Pay particular attention to repetitions of (i) individual words and (ii) sequences of words.

        This can reveal a preoccupying idea on your part—which may or may not be valid. Decide about this (e.g. 'murder', 'planned', 'patriot') occurring on the note.

    (b) Note the sequence of your ideas. It may reveal a relationship perceived by your mind—again, which may or may not be valid. Try to understand the sequences. The student who completed the note on Stalinist Russia tends to see things in negative terms and is moralistic.

    (c) Consider also the quantity of information in front of you. It is quite usual to be pleasantly surprised by the large amount of information that has been produced, even on a subject you may feel ignorant or confused about. It can thus have a considerable therapeutic value!

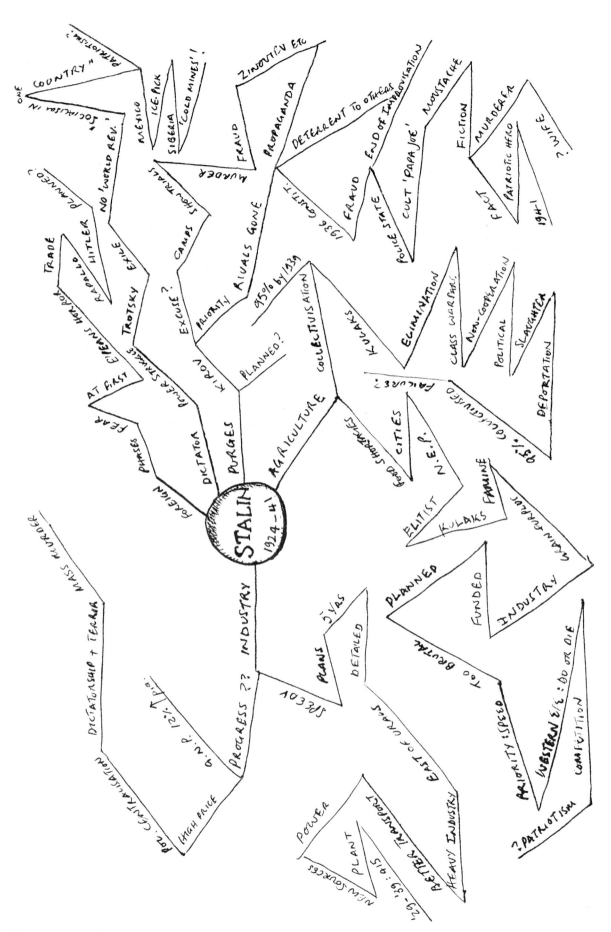

QUESTIONS

Study the two diagrams (1) and (2) below:

1. What are the weaknesses of the diagrams in terms of:
   (a) design
   e.g. the apparent inevitability of a 'road' to power.
   (b) details
   e.g. how important were economic factors in the success of Mussolini's bid for supreme power?

2. Does anything else need to be added to diagrams (1) and (2)? What considerations influence your decisions?

3. What advantages and disadvantages do diagrammatic notes have in comparison with your usual linear notes?

   How could you successfully represent the three tasks mentioned above by using linear notes?

(1)

MUSSOLINI'S ROAD TO POWER

(2)

MUSSOLINI'S ACCESSION

EXAMPLE: THE EASTERN QUESTION

Below are some examples of how the different note-systems might be applied to a specific topic. They are intended to complement one another and provide an element of variety for the note-maker.

They also offered a challenge to the note-maker at *an early stage* when the student was forced to analyse and assimilate information *before* beginning to make file-notes.

Compare these notes with the earlier efforts by a different student on p.41.

A.

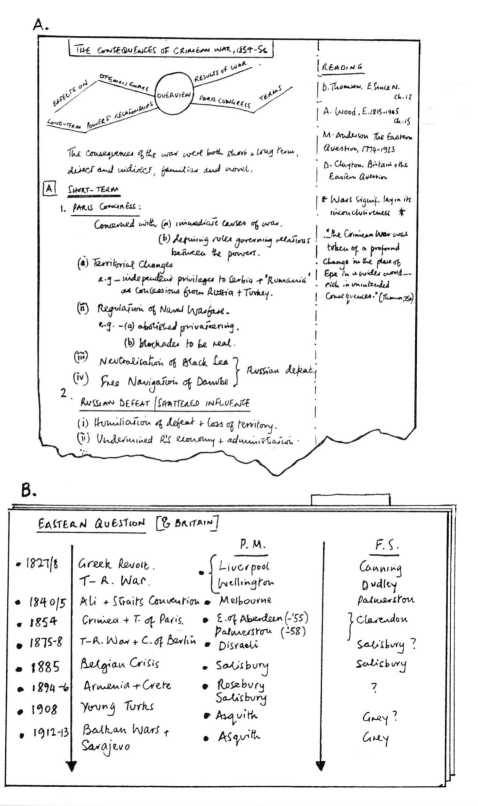

B.

C.

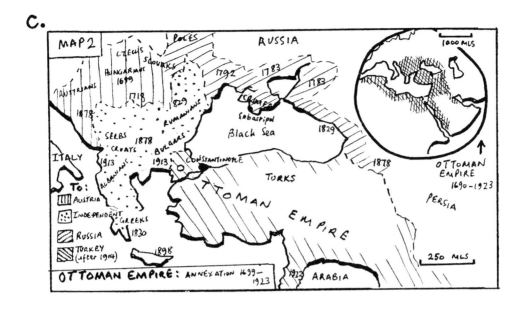

D.

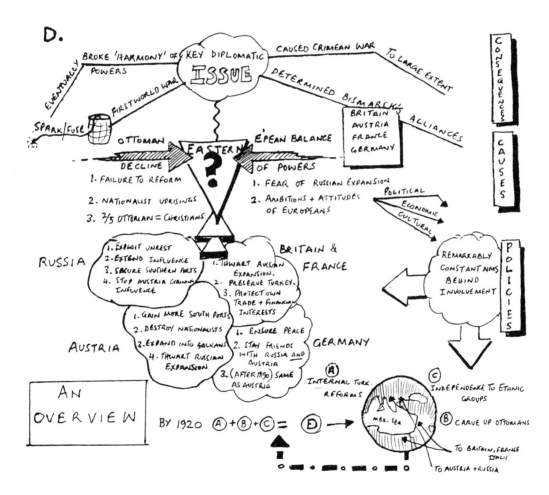

USE A VARIETY OF NOTE-METHODS
FOR THE SAME TOPIC

E. A SUMMARY OF METHODS AND USES

NOTE-MAKING METHOD	APPROPRIATE ACTIVITY	MAIN ADVANTAGES	POSSIBLE DISADVANTAGES
PATTERN	1. Analysis of topics. 2. Essay planning. 3. Revision summaries. 4. Lesson/Lecture notes.	1. Memorable. 2. Interesting/creative. 3. Analytical and structured. 4. Concise and relevant. 5. Organic.	1. Unfamiliar at first. 2. Messy and awkward for novice. 3. No room for great amount of factual detail.
LINEAR	1. Chronological and descriptive narratives. 2. Quotations. 3. Essay drafts.	1. Great quantities of detail can be recorded. 2. Thinking can be expressed in full verbal form—vocabulary and style can be developed.	1. May discourage proper analysis and organisation. 2. Key ideas tend to be hidden behind superfluous vocabulary and irrelevant detail.
DIAGRAMS AND TABLES	1. Summary accounts. 2. Analysis of topics. 3. Statistical information. 4. Maps.	1. Can reveal sequences of information. 2. Can show interconnections between events and ideas. 3. Memorable.	1. Danger of over-simplification and historical distortion. 2. Some devices disguise as much as they reveal.
CARDS	1. Glossary. 2. Biographical index. 3. Revision aid. 4. Research for essays, etc.	1. Can be easily rearranged according to need. 2. Encourage brevity and conciseness.	1. Only carry limited amount of information. 2. No overall framework can be seen.
SPIDER	1. Revision/recall. 2. Essay planning. 3. Group 'brainstorming'.	1. Encourages flow of information. 2. Can provide reassurance over amount of information.	1. Incoherence may be off-putting. 2. Cannot provide a record of ideas and information.

F. CHECKLIST

1. Try to experiment (more than once!) with each of the different note-making methods.

2. Analyse why you prefer particular methods. Do you think your reasons are valid?

3. Do you use your notes for developing your historical understanding as well as for recording historical information?

4. Learn to recognise the difference between analysis of historical events and mere description in your note-making system.

5. Try to identify the main ideas in your notes and distinguish these from (a) subordinate ideas and (b) supporting or illustrative information.

6. Learn how to distill large quantities of information into their bare essentials.

7. Are important ideas transformed into key-recall words by you?

8. Ensure that you review and revise your notes periodically in the light of new knowledge and increased understanding.

QUESTION ANALYSIS

About this Chapter

This chapter deals with the problem of understanding historical questions. It concentrates on questions set as essay titles. It assumes that the question will be considered with a basic knowledge of the topic. Various methods or tools of analysis are proposed and explained. Whilst not infallible, such tools should encourage a more critical approach and greater understanding of the question.

A. THE IMPORTANCE OF QUESTION ANALYSIS

'Candidates do need firmer guidance and practice in examination techniques as fundamental as reading carefully the examination questions, noting the emphasis given by the wording generally to any particular word or phrase and deciding what particular response the question invites, so that a more discerning and discriminating attitude may be adopted to shaping the material to hand to meet the needs of specific questions.'

(J.M.B. Examiners' Report: A level History, 1981, p.22)

Question analysis involves:

(a) appreciating the type of question.
(b) examining the parts of the question.
(c) understanding the significance of a question.
(d) developing a line of argument in response to the question.

Question analysis is a fundamental skill for Advanced level students of History.

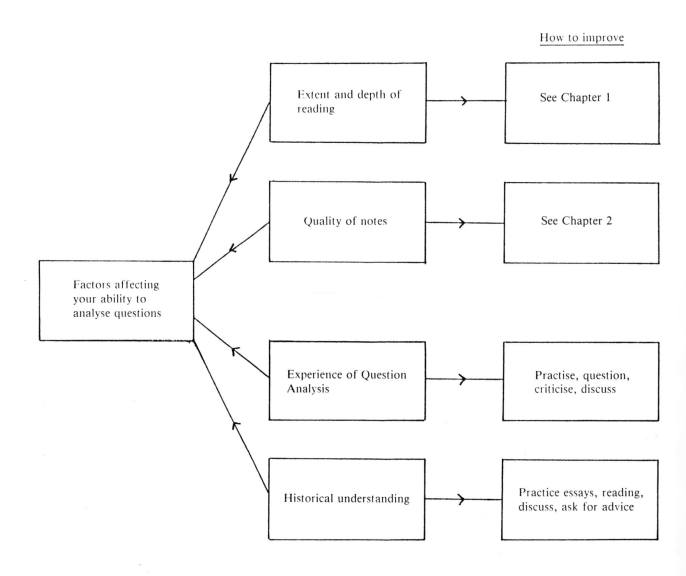

How to improve

Extent and depth of reading	→	See Chapter 1
Quality of notes	→	See Chapter 2
Experience of Question Analysis	→	Practise, question, criticise, discuss
Historical understanding	→	Practice essays, reading, discuss, ask for advice

Factors affecting your ability to analyse questions

B. THE PURPOSE OF QUESTIONS AT ADVANCED LEVEL

Understanding what questions are designed to do will help us answer them. The examination is a collection of questions and individually a question goes some way to satisfying the requirements of the examination.

The Joint Matriculation Board (J.M.B.) state four things to be tested at Advanced level.

SUMMARY OF OBJECTIVES:
(a) 'the knowledge and understanding of factual material.'
(b) 'the ability to draw conclusions from historical evidence.'
(c) 'the ability to evaluate opinions.'
(d) 'the ability to *select* and *organise relevant knowledge . . . to analyse and answer specific* historical questions.'

These objectives are largely the same for all Advanced level examinations. The words which are emphasised are vital for understanding question analysis and essay writing.

Notice that:

1. the order of the objectives reveals something of the process of historical writing. The historian starts with some knowledge or facts (a), adds opinion, interpretations, judgements, (b) and (c) and presents them in a logical and relevant essay (d). The last of these objectives is most important, since understanding it will make the difference between good and bad essays or grades.

2. marks are awarded in line with these objectives. Firstly, some credit will be given for knowledge. Every essay must have a solid foundation of factual knowledge. You cannot avoid reading and making notes to provide a fund of knowledge on which to draw. Secondly, knowledge is not the only thing that is important in a good essay, 'wholly narrative answers (factual or story telling) will be restricted to a maximum of 10 marks out of the 25 available for an individual question'. Allowing for your knowledge being detailed and accurate that gives a maximum of 40%—a bare pass.

> 'Every question asked requires historical information to be applied: the basic need here is for the candidate to *select* information which is *relevant* and to *organise* it in such a way that it is directed towards answering the specific question asked.'
> (London University Examiners' Report: A level History, 1981, p.359)

Most of the marks will be awarded for demonstrating more sophisticated skills, that is to say for analysis, judgement, interpretation and assessment of knowledge. *Mastery* of the information must be proved by *marshalling* it, that is in the way you select and organise information relevant to the question.

For this reason you are *not* asked questions which would require *only* knowledge, as this would be solely a test of memory. Advanced level questions, therefore, do not begin 'What happened in . . .' or 'Describe the events of . . .'

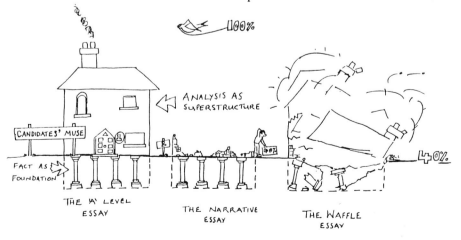

C. QUESTIONING THE QUESTION

Despite any impression you may have gained, History is not just concerned with finding the answers. One of the fundamental skills of the historian is the ability to ask questions. In this chapter we will concentrate on generating questions. *You must have a critical frame of mind for all historical work.* Being critical means that you must question any information, material or statement you come across to test and establish its meaning and truth. The idea of questioning is central to the chapters on reading, notemaking and documentary evidence.

Questioning does not take place only with essays or their titles. When faced with a document, gobbet, quotation, exercise or problem, do not accept it passively, but interrogate it thoroughly. Historical work is a two-way process—a dialogue between the historian and his evidence. You will find that being actively involved in this dialogue is interesting and enjoyable. You will also find that to generate the right question is usually more difficult than to find the right answer.

The questions which are tackled at Advanced level reflect the many aspects and problems of History as a subject.

D. THE LOGIC OF QUESTIONS: PROBLEMS AND TYPES

The Problems of History

The problems of the historian mark his subject out from other disciplines. When combined and presented *in an Advanced level question it is difficult to see the underlying historical problems. You must reach behind the form or wording of the question, dismantle it and carefully examine each part.*

SOME OF THE SKILLS OF HISTORY	SOME OF THE PROBLEMS OF HISTORY	EXAMPLES
Understand Judge Be Aware of Explain Define Assess Appreciate Analyse	Human motivation, aims and values	J. Chamberlain D. Lloyd-George
	Success or failure/ achievement	Unification of Italy Chartism The General Strike 1926
	Continuity (not always obvious)	Versailles, Weimar and the Rise of Hitler British Foreign Policy 1815–65
	Change	Social impact of First World War Russian Revolution 1917
	Change and continuity	Whig Reform in 1830's Disraelian conservatism
	Movements, large forces, abstractions	Nazism Socialism Chartism Bourgeosie Appeasement
	Terms and ideas	Imperiaslism, Nationalism Fascism Revolution Laissez-faire Cold War
	Influence or work of individuals/ institutions in isolation and on the whole	Bismarck, Peel Palmerston The Fabians
	Parts and whole of a policy or period	Irish Question in British politics The Congress system
	Debates between historians	'War Guilt' Decline of Liberal Party Origins of Second World War

A RANGE OF QUESTIONS (1815–1951)

1. *Account for the emergence and failure of the Paris Commune 1871.*

2. *Consider the extent to which colonial rivalry was a cause of the First World War.*

3. *With what success did Alexander II deal with problems Russia faced during his reign?*

4. *Account for the dominance of Prussia in Germany by 1867.*

5. *Examine the impact of the Second World War on the civilian populations of Europe.*

6. 'Chartism was the product and victim of economic circumstances'. Discuss.

7. 'British politicians never really understood the Eastern Question'. To what extent is this view substantiated by British foreign policy 1854 to 1878?

8. 'Limited but useful'. Discuss the validity of the assessment of Disraeli's social reforms 1874-80.

9. How far was the political crisis 1909-11 made inevitable by the Liberal victory in 1906?

10. To what extent were politicians responsible for the high unemployment which Britain experienced between the wars?

Question Types

The first approach that may be used in breaking down questions is to look for the question types. There are two basic question types.

(a) EXPLANATION TYPE—	(giving reasons for something)
(b) ASSESSMENT/EVALUATION TYPE—(weighing up something and saying how fair, sensible, reasonable or true it is)	

Notice that many questions will be a combination of these two types.

Examples of question type

(a) EXPLANATION
'Why was Britain so slow to develop a national system of education before 1914?

(b) ASSESSMENT/EVALUATION
'The period 1880-1914 witnessed a revolution in English education! How true is this statement?'

(c) EXPLANATION AND ASSESSMENT
'What were the problems which faced Stalin on his accession to power and how successfully did he resolve them?

You decide the question type by concentrating on what we shall call the 'instruction part' of the question. In this part the instructions are given before the question or the problem is set. The wording of the instruction will usually be the clue to the type of question.

The Instruction Parts of Questions

EXPLANATION (WHY?) QUESTIONS	EVALUATION OR ASSESSMENT QUESTIONS
Why . . .	To what extent . . .
Account for . . .	Estimate the value of . . ./the importance of . . .
What do you understand by . . .	Assess the influence of . . .
Outline the . . .	In what respect was . . ./what ways did . . .
Why did . . ./	How successful/satisfactorily . . .
Why didn't . . ./weren't . . ./wasn't . . .	How far do you accept the view/judgement . . .
What problems faced . . .	Compare the contribution/value of . . .
Explain the course of . . .	What significance . . ./justification . . ./contribution . . ./part . . .
What were the aims . . .	Consider the validity of . . .
What factors . . ./considerations . . .	With what justification . . ./success . . .
In what ways . . .	What was the importance
Discuss the nature of . . ./	Evaluate the . . .
the part played by . . .	How true . . ./effective . . ./successful . . .
Examine the role of . . .	Describe and assess the . . .
Comment on the . . .	Discuss the verdict . . ./the view that . . ./observation that . . ./
	this statement . . ./the comment . . ./the importance of . . .
	Examine the claim that . . .
	Comment on the . . .

Look at the questions on p.67–68 and see how these 'clues' help you to analyse questions.

We have made a simple beginning to question analysis. This division into explanation and assessment is not rigid. Because:

1. many questions are a combination of the two types.

   e.g. *'what problems faced (the Bolsheviks in 1917) and*

   explanation

   how satisfactorily were they resolved by 1924?

   assessment

2. the rest of the question may shift the emphasis from explanation to assessment. You could perhaps, be asked to assess the value and strength of an explanation.

e.g. *'How far can the origins of (the First World War in 1914) be explained by German policy from 1898?*

assessment

E. ANALYSIS BY PART:
THE WORDING OF QUESTIONS

To dismantle the question further look for the other parts.

1. The instruction part .... _____

2. The main topic .... [   ]

3. The key factor, phrase or words   **bold**

Use a different colour or symbol to identify each part of your question.

A. Consider the **importance for Russia of** Stalin's policies in the period 1927 to 1939.

B. How influential in securing the repeal of the Corn Laws were the **activities of the Anti-Corn Law League?**

C. **'Tragic and unnecessary'.** Comment on the origins of the Boer War in the light of this statement.

D. Account for the **industrial and political** unrest witnessed in the years 1909 to 1914

Paraphrasing the Question

Having analysed the parts of a question take and rephrase the question, using your own words and concentrating on the key factor, phrase or word of the title. For example:

Question A—
concentrates on assessing the significance or importance for Russia of Stalin's policies between 1927 and 1939.

Question B—
focuses on assessing the role, power, part, importance of the Anti-Corn Law League in bringing about the repeal of the Corn Laws.

Question C—
focuses on 'tragic' and 'unnecessary' as valid, fair assessments of the causes of the Boer War.

Question D—
focuses on explaining the reasons for the industrial and political unrest in Britain in the five years before the outbreak of the First World War.

(Notice in our paraphrase that the key factor, phrase or words is the first thing we refer to. We give it proper attention by placing it first).

Try to paraphrase the questions on p.67–68.

HOW WILL THIS HELP?

1. The key factor, phrase or word is more important than the main topic.

2. Paraphrasing brings the key factor, phrase or word of the question to the surface and forces you to answer it, not write about the main topic.

3. You will be inclined to more relevance in the examination. It will discourage the all too common, careless 'triggering' of a response (usually chronological and narrative) to a few familiar words.

4. Paraphrasing should tell you whether you can answer the question. Too often students look for any excuse—a familiar form of words as the main topic—to relieve themselves of a mass of factual information.

F. UNDERSTANDING THE QUESTION: IMPLICATIONS

In order to proceed with your analysis and understand the question fully, you will need to look for what is 'hidden' in and by the question. You need to be able to understand what the question is telling you about itself. Questions will imply certain things about the way you should answer them. By *imply* we mean that something is being *suggested indirectly*. There are two ways in which the question implies something about itself:

(a) in what it selects from or assumes about an historical problem.

(b) in requiring the measurement or weighing up of an historical problem.

To recognise implications you may need a little knowledge of the topic, so familiarise yourself with the information by reading your notes or textbooks. Searching for the implications of a question is beginning to relate your knowledge to a specific question.

Selection and Assumptions

We will use the process of question analysis already shown to dismantle this question.

'How far was the decline of the Liberal party 1906–24 due to the rise of the Labour Party?'

Question type:
(a) the question part asks for assessment 'How far were . . .'
(b) but the words 'due to' change the emphasis to explanation
(c) we are dealing with assessing the validity of an explanation

Question parts:
Instruction part: 'How far was . . . due to'
Main topic: 'the Liberal party'
Key factor, phrase or word: 'the decline of . . . the rise of the Labour party 1906–24'.

Paraphrase:
The question focuses on the rise of the Labour party 1906–24 as a reason for the decline of the Liberal party.

The question assumes that there is a connection between the key phrase and the main topic and our knowledge should tell us if this is a reasonable assumption. The implication can be seen by thinking of the instruction part and the key phrase or word. *There may be other ways of explaining the decline of the Liberal party in this period.* Liberalism may have declined because of:

(a) **the impact of the First World War**
(b) **its failure to properly undertake social reform**
(c) **lack of success in dealing with the Irish question**
(d) **long-term structural changes in the British economy**
(e) **dissonance between 'old' and 'new' Liberalism etc.**

You could substitute any of these alternative explanations as the key factor or phrase in the question e.g.

How far was the decline of the Liberal party, 1906–24, due to **the impact of the First World War?**

or **the split in its leadership**?
or **the failure of social reform**?
or **lack of success in dealing with the Irish question**?

So you could go on reviewing and reworking the problem. Just as the key factor or phrase may be changed so the rest of the wording of the question could alter, but the basic form of the problem remains the same.

Note that all these questions:

1. *Assume* that there is a connection between the main topic (the decline of the Liberal Party 1906–24) and the key factor named.

2. *Select* one key factor to highlight in relation to the main topic and do not mention the others.

3. *Imply* by their wording that the factor named is not the only one that needs mentioning.

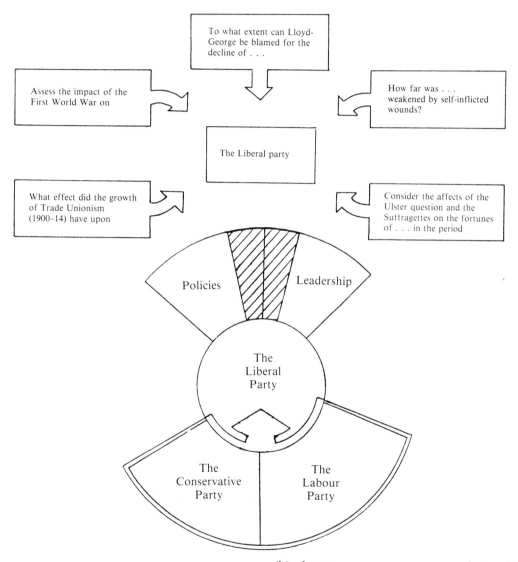

Notice

(a) that some parts or aspects of a topic may be strongly connected or overlap. Both the information required and the question may suggest this.

Which proved more influential for the Liberal party before 1914, its policies or its leadership?

(b) that some parts or aspects of a topic naturally lend themselves to comparisons or joint treatment. The question may acknowledge this.

Compare the respective contributions of the Conservative party and of the Labour party to the decline of the Liberal party (1906–29).

(c) some questions will require an overview of a topic.

'in government in 1914; in ruins in 1930'. How do you explain the decline of the Liberal party?

Think of this common form of question as a *'part and whole'*. *Part* of the topic or problem (the ambition of the princes) has been selected. The question is designed to see how well you understand the significance of that *part* in relation to the *whole* topic (explaining the decline of the Liberal party 1906-24). If you do not recognise that the question is implying that something has been selected, you will only answer a part and not the whole of it. The implication of our question is that we cannot explain the decline of the Liberal party unless we mention the other factors. We must do justice to *all* the factors involved.

Assessment

Frequently questions demand assessment or evaluation. In a broad division on p. 70 we separated explanation from assessment type questions by examining their instruction parts. This is a somewhat crude tool of analysis. Some assessment questions are obvious: mention of success, failure, achievement or significance are all clues that some sort of weighing up is needed. But in some questions it is not obvious what you are assessing; it is implied.

Armed with your knowledge of how to relate the parts and the whole, it is possible to see implied assessment. Consider our question 'How far was the decline of the Liberal party 1906-24 due to the rise of the Labour party?'. We recognise that a collection of factors explain the decline of the Liberal party 1906-24. The instruction 'How far was . . . due to' implies assessment of *the relative importance* of those factors. In other words, were some factors e.g. the rise of Labour, more or less important than others, e.g. the First World War?

Look at the different requirements and forms of assessment in the following questions.

QUESTION	TYPE	COMMENTARY
1. *Account for the decline of the Liberal party 1906-24*	Explanation	1. You have to present the factors which explain the decline of the Liberal party in the specific period. A better candidate would wish to attach some 'priority' to these factors, quickly showing an understanding of their relative importance and influence at different times.
2. *How do you account for the decline of the Liberal party to 1924? To what extent had this process started before 1914?*	Explanation and Assessment	2. As for Question 1. but in this example you are asked to assess how far the process of decline had gone before 1914, if as some historians maintain, it had started at all!
3. *To what extent were the Liberal party in decline before 1914?*	Assessment	3. This is the latter half of Question 2. and makes a sophisticated question standing on its own. It would assume that Question 1. be briefly or implicitly answered as a part of the assessment.
4. *Assess the impact of the First World War on the Liberal party.*	Assessment	4. In this question one factor is concentrated on. It is clear that an assessment of the impact of one factor (the First World War) upon the Liberal party is required.
5. *What was the most important factor in the decline of the Liberal party?*	Assessment	5. Here you are clearly asked to decide on 'the important factor'. This question focuses directly on the relative importance of parts of a whole. It assumes that the decline of the Liberal party may be explained by more than one factor.
6. *How important a factor was the First World War in weakening the Liberal party?*	Assessment	6. The most difficult question of the six. Unlike Question 5. where you are clearly asked for the relative importance of problems, this question *implies* that the First World War may be more or less important than factors in weakening the Liberals. In a sense the question 'disguises' or implies that assessment of the first World War in weakening the Liberals must be in relation to other factors.

Both of the following questions imply assessment of relative importance. What suggests this in the question? Of what are you assessing the relative importance?

1. *How far was combating socialism the prime motive for the Liberal social reforms 1906–14?*

2. *Examine the view that the rise of the Labour party was largely due to the changes in the Coal Industry 1889–1924.*

There are similar implications in some of the questions on p.67. See if you can find them.

Assessment forms a large part of historical work. In every question needing assessment a standard or scale of reference is required by which you can measure relative success, failure or achievement. In each case the standard used should be realistic for the time or period which you are studying. Thus, it is all too easy to see in the Liberal social reforms before 1914, the beginning of the Welfare State. However, in the search for origins employing such a term as Welfare State may obscure a real understanding of what the individuals at the time intended or what they created. Similarly, however much we may disapprove of the Nazis judging Hitler to be evil is not a satisfactory historical explanation.

We said earlier that it was important to generate questions. The final stages of analysis must be to see what questions the analysis suggests. At this stage you must use your knowledge and apply it to the question and its information content.

These tools of analysis are not always necessary or infallible. The questions may be simple enough not to require the application of the whole process. Whatever analysis you do will give important direction to the construction of an argument at the planning stage of essay writing.

G. THE INFORMATION CONTENT IN QUESTIONS

Consider these questions:

1. *'Less a response to political pressure, more good economic sense'. Discuss this view of the origins of the Liberal social reforms 1906–14.*

2. *Examine the origins of the Liberal social reforms, 1906–14.*

The first may seem more difficult than the second. Questions which include dates, quotations and complex wording are initially offputting. Long quotations with the cheerless instruction; 'Discuss', often provoke much puzzlement and feeble answers. It is natural for the student to prefer a more straightforward wording and form. However, some of the most formidable-looking questions can be the most ordinary and helpful titles.

1. Complex questions can be simple tasks in disguise.

2. The more information in a question, the more you are helped to understand its meaning and needs.

3. You only need more patience to unravel a complexly worded question, not necessarily more ability.

Questions with a high and specific information content give you more to go on. You have an early line of argument provided by the question. In our first example you are guided by the ideas of 'political pressure' or 'economic' reasons as a cause and emphasis is given to the latter. In the second question you must provide assessment and argument for yourself; there is a lower information content. There are two ways of looking at this more general question: it is either an opportunity or a trap. It is an opportunity in offering flexibility to the writer to construct his or her own line of argument and range of discussion. It is a trap in that, without early guidelines or help, the writer will ramble, addressing the topic not the question. Neither a high or low information content nor general or specific essay title is to be preferred, but to understand their potential is vital.

Words

You will find that certain words have a significant meaning for the topic or subject matter you are examining. Such words can hide a wealth of meaning.

1. Some words apply to a wider historical debate e.g. 'Victorianism', 'New Imperialism', 'Great Depression', 'Scramble for Africa', 'War

73

Guilt', 'Cold War'. They are used as a piece of shorthand by historians. Treat these words with care; take the time and effort to understand and explain them.

2. Be aware of the ethical or prejudicial value of words. You must isolate or note the bias and loading of words like 'Tyranny', 'just', 'misguided', 'blame'.

3. A word can carry the whole meaning of a question e.g. 'opportunist', 'inevitable', 'substantial', 'decisive', 'influence', 'comprehensive' etc.

Never accept any of these words unquestioningly. A sentence spent defining a word or phrase can make valid the rest of your answer.

EXAMPLE

'The Period 1880–1914 witnessed a revolution in English education'. How true is this statement?	*Why was Britain so slow to develop a national system of education before 1914?*
QUESTION TYPE (QT)	QUESTION TYPE (QT)
Assessment 'How true is . . . a revolution'	Explanation 'why'
QUESTION PARTS (QP)	QUESTION PARTS (QP)
Instruction(I) 'How true is this statement' Main topic (MT) 'English education 1880–1914' Key phrase/word (KP/W) 'a revolution'	(I) 'why was' (MT) Development of British education before 1914 (KP/W) 'so slow'
PARAPHRASE	PARAPHRASE
The question focuses on the 'revolutionary' nature of change in English education	Focuses on the speed (lack of it/slowness) in the development of British Education before 1914.
UNDERSTANDING	UNDERSTANDING
Dates confine the discussion 1870–1914. Mundella's Act 1880 made education compulsory. 'Revolution' is key judgement. Failure to discriminate different branches of education.	The important word is 'slow' to describe the pace of change/development in English education and implies that it ought to have been quicker.
1. For whom was it revolutionary—government/state, recipients, churches? 2. Was the revolution 'complete' by 1914? 3. What change pre-1880? 1870 Act. 4. How significant was 1902 Act for change? 5. Were all forms of education (elementary, secondary, technical) changed? To the same extent? 6. What qualitative change occurred? Intended/unintended consequences?	1. Why was it held back? 2. What held it back? How did these factors work together? 3. When did it begin to change more rapidly? Is slow a fair assessment for this whole period? 4. Why did change come when it did?

Quotations

Quotations should not be a problem. If the words used are unusual, difficult or technical, find out from a dictionary or your teacher, what they mean. Crucially you are trying to understand the whole sense of the quotation or question, so do not forget the overall effect of individual words.

Ask of each quotation 'What job is it doing?' For example, does it judge, explain, assess, describe or interpret a point in relation to the topic?

Quotations conform to the same pattern of assessment and explanation type. They may be analysed using the same tools—looking for question parts (main topic, instruction, key phrase/word), appreciating selection and implications.

Notice in the next examples:

1. the quotations help by increasing the information content of the question.

2. the simplicity and vagueness of the alternative question leaves a lot for the writer to provide.

3. the quotations themselves give way to analysis.

'less a response to political pressure, more good economic sense'. Discuss this view of the origins of the Liberal social reforms 1906-1914.
 	
QUESTION TYPE
 	
Assessment (of an explanation) 'Discuss this view . . ./less political . . ./more economic . . .'
 	
QUESTION PARTS
 	
(I) Discuss this view
(MT) Liberal social reforms 1904-14
(KP/W) 'less . . . political pressure, more . . . economic'
 	
PARAPHRASE
 	
Focuses on economic considerations rather than political motives for passing of social reform legislation by the Liberal governments 1906-14
 	
UNDERSTANDING
 	
1. Where did political pressure come from? How was it expressed?
2. In what sense economic? Macro-national economy?
3. Did political pressure affect certain reforms? Economic considerations? Others?
4. Who had an economic stake in these matters?
5. Other reasons apart from political/economic e.g.
    ideological/social justice
    institutional
    individuals
	Examine the origins of the Liberal social reforms 1906-1914
	
	QUESTION TYPE
	
	Explanation/assessment 'Examine'
	
	QUESTION PARTS
	
	(I) Examine
	(MT) Liberal social reforms 1906-1914
	(KP/W) Origins
	
	PARAPHRASE
	
	The question focuses on the motives, beginnings of the Liberal social reforms 1906-1914
	
	UNDERSTANDING
	
	1. Why were they introduced?
	2. Why then?
	3. What caused them to take the form they did?

'idealist and radical'. How true is this view of Joseph Chamberlain's contribution to developments in the British Empire? QUESTION TYPE Assessment 'how true is this view' QUESTION PARTS (I) 'How true is this view' (MT) Joseph Chamberlain and Empire (KP/W) 'idealist', 'radical' PARAPHRASE Focuses on validity of 'radical' and 'idealist' to describe Joseph Chamberlain's involvement with the British Empire. UNDERSTANDING 1. Contrast what J. Chamberlain did with his motives and ideals 2. What did he do which was new, different? Why was it different? Was it 'radical'? 3. How practical were the solutions he offered? 'Idealist' seems critical, why might this be so?	*Evaluate the policies and achievements of Joseph Chamberlain.* QUESTION TYPE Assessment 'evaluate' QUESTION PARTS (I) Evaluate (MT) Joseph Chamberlain (KP/W) 'policies and achievements' PARAPHRASE Focuses on the policies and achievements of Joseph Chamberlain UNDERSTANDING 1. Which activity merits the term 'achievement'?

Look at the questions on p.67–68. What is the purpose of the quotations in the questions? How much information do they give? Can you find or suggest a quotation for those without one? What would it have to do?

Your understanding of the question will be based on:

(a) your analysis into types and parts.
(b) your paraphrases.
(c) the implication of selection or assessment.
(d) the information content (of the question itself).
(e) your own knowledge (of topic).

Further questions are generated by the interaction of these five factors.

THE PROCESS OF QUESTION ANALYSIS			
Stages	Headings Analysis	Activity	Product
1.	Question type	(a) Locate instructions part. (b) Examine overall effect of question.	(i) Assessment. (ii) Explanation
2.	Question parts	Separate and code by colour or symbol.	Instructions. Main topic. Key phrase/word. Remainder.
3.	Paraphrase	(a) Use your own words where possible. (b) Focus on key phrase/word.	Highlight key phrase/word.
4.	Understanding	(a) Recognise whole and parts. (b) Look for implied assessment. (c) Look for a wider or hidden meaning.	Isolates and examines. Selection, assumptions. Information content; —wording —quotations.
5.	Further Questions	(a) What further questions are suggested by the above analysis? (b) Relate your knowledge to the question.	How to proceed with the questions.

A Question Analysis model

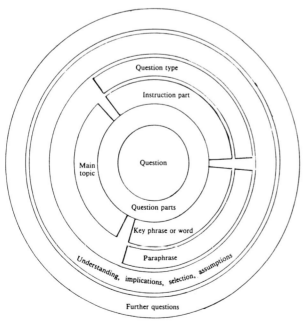

You can use the process of analysis with this model. Place your question in the centre of the model and work outwards from the parts to the further questions.

H. A LINE OF ARGUMENT: ASSEMBLING THE ANSWER

Having analysed and come to an understanding of the question, you have to build an argument from it. This will be a series of reasoned, relevant points made in much the same way as a lawyer presents a case in a court of law, though your case will not be as one-sided as a lawyer's and your judge will be the reader or teacher!

You must overcome the difficulty of abundant information by concentrating on your *basic response* to the question or the *main line of argument*. You will be *using* the idea of a main argument or basic response to help direct your thoughts and *contain* the argument. The main argument method is like a set of blinkers for a horse in a race, forcing a straight line and avoiding distractions. Lawyers work from a main argument. Everything presented to the court is designed to support their basic argument of either guilt or innocence. So set yourself the task of suggesting a simple argument or answer and then you can try to make out a case for it.

SOME POSSIBLE ESSAY QUESTIONS AND POSSIBLE ANSWERS.

1. *How far was the decline of the Liberal party 1906–24 due to the rise of the Labour party?*

Suggested answers/argument:
Yes, after the Franchise Act 1918 (1918–24), not so before.
or: No, long-term economic and social changes led to Liberal decline and Labour's rise.
or: No, the Liberals were responsible for their own decline.

2. *'The period 1870–1914 witnessed a revolution in English education'. How true is this statement?*

Suggested answers/argument:
Yes, a revolution.
or: No, such changes had long been coming and were incomplete by 1914.

3. *Why was Britain so slow to develop a national system of education before 1914?*

Suggested answers/argument:
Because of religious opposition.
or: Because the need was not recognised.

4. *Examine the origins of the Liberal social reforms 1906–14.*

Suggested answers/argument:
Origins lay in political changes of 19th century—franchise, Labour etc.
or: Origins lay in need to maintain growth of capitalist economy.

5. *'Idealist and radical'. How true is this view of Joseph Chamberlain's contribution to developments in the British Empire?*

Suggested answers/argument:
Yes, both terms apply.
or: No, neither satisfactorily explains his lack of real achievement in Imperial affairs.

The main argument or basic responses you have been searching for are short statements which represent a stance or attitude to the question. It has been called a 'gut' response. *It is the essence of your answer.* It may be that you have chosen a difficult argument to support or defend. You will find that out as you arrange the information or evidence to back it up.

Again limit yourself this time to the six (more or less if necessary) most important reasons or pieces of evidence which support your suggested answer.

1. *How far was the decline of the Liberal party 1906–24 due to the rise of the Labour party?*

Main line of argument: no necessary connection, decline due to long-term social/economic forces and First World War.

(a)/(b) Weakening of traditional Liberal support,
e.g. Welsh nonconformity, Irish nationalism, religious influence less especially in urban areas, failure to support working class M.P.s, weak provincial organization.
Old Liberalism, 'new' Liberalism/social reform.

(c) Economic/social changes,
e.g. changes in ind. organization—concentration/new management, long-term trends to change economy—esp. staple industries, 'vertical' deference makes way for horizontal class-based politics post.
Population mobility/change.

(d) Increased support for Labour,
e.g. Legal actions vs. Trade Unions, increase in Unionism
1901 Miners Federation decision.
Strong local associations
Spread of Socialist *ideas* to certain key groups in working class.

(e) Impact of First World War,
e.g. political split in Liberals, attack on Liberal values.
economic effects e.g. coal
1918 election
1918 franchise decision
effect on Labour party

(f) Strength of Conservatism,
e.g. attracting lower middle class.

In this assessment of an explanation the writer has disagreed with the main proposition and supported it by looking at the Liberal and Labour parties separately, and secondly at the other factors making for Liberal decline. At the same time as writing down the reasons, other things came to mind which could illustrate and support those reasons, so they are jotted down too.

3. *Why was Britain so slow to develop a national system of education before 1914?*

Main line of argument: because of forces resistant to change, e.g. principally religious, also economic. Need and realisation came from political/economic changes, pace changed after 1870. Kay-Shuttleworth/Graham 1843. Cowper-Temple clause. National Passive Resistance Comm.

(a) Religious influence retarded the speed of change (NEL/NEU (2 para?)

(b) Economic and social pressures impeded the efficient working of the system—part-time workers, poorer rural areas could not afford educ., illness of public health, cost of full provision.

(c) There were structural and institutional obstacles to overcome—competing authorities, many local rates and 1902 Act. Within educational provision background of teaching/personnel, payment by results/limited curriculum.

(d) Political and intellectual ideas changed—political/national/social, educated electorate 1867, 1884. Decline of 'Laissez faire' ideas e.g. P. Health. Humanity, Huxeley's "ladder".

(e) Social and economic forces brought about the possiblity and need for change—1870, Boom period, education could be afforded, educated workforce, international econ. rivalry, improve morality, behaviour, social order. Child psychology/youth.

All of these points explain religious and economic resistance to state education and the ideas which forces change; together they explain the slow pace of educational development.

In order to make all of these main points work in an essay you can think of the reasons you have found as questions for yourself, and answer each with a paragraph. Thus, for the question about the slow pace of educational change you could set a paragraph to answer the following questions. Compare them with the main reasons supporting the argument.

(i) How and why did religious influences affect education? What examples of this influence can be found? How were they overcome?

(ii) In what ways did economic factors impede progress, initially and during the period?

(iii) What other factors retarded the pace of change? How were they overcome?

(iv) Which ideas encouraged change? When? (change of pace?)

(v) How did changes in society and the economy bring about the need for educational change?

Notice that each paragraph question could be worthy of fuller treatment (i.e. an essay title) in its own right. This reveals the importance of flexibility and familiarity in revision. You need an active revision system which allows you to adjust your knowledge to different questions. It is described more fully in the Revision chapter.

The process takes a little time to grasp but very soon you will quickly put down on paper a series of 'main points'. You may then think of them as questions for each paragraph to answer. By framing questions for each paragrah you are giving your reasons a place in the argument, and specifying a job for each paragraph to do.

In the essay all you have to do is answer the question for each paragraph!

How important a part of the Nazi popular appeal before 1933 was their anti-semitism?

QUESTION TYPE
Assessment 'How important'

QUESTION PARTS

(I) How important a part
(MT) the Nazis before 1933
(KP/W) 'Popular appeal . . . anti-semitism'

PARAPHRASE

Focuses on anti-semitism as a factor in making Nazism attractive.

UNDERSTANDING

1. Difficult question, the date 1933 is important and does not include their record when in power.
2. Other factors may be more significant in explaining their appeal.
3. On what was this appeal based?

ANSWER/ARGUMENT

In accounting for the popular appeal of the Nazis, anti-semitism was not as significant as other factors, especially that of Hitler himself.

REASONS

1. Most German people were not attracted to Nazism because of its anti-semitism. It was part of a racial package (Volk, Aryan etc.) supplied by the Nazis. Jews were a small proportion of the population.

2. Hitler's personality was the most influential and the 'saviour' idea.

3. The Nazi party machine and its presentation was impressive—Youth, S.A., militarism, order, ideology, violence.

4. Nazi propaganda/programme = wide appeal.

5. Economic circumstances provided a context for Nazi appeal. Reaction to Versailles/Weimar also helped.

QUESTIONS

Para 1. Was anti-semitism an issue in the past? How important was it in Nazism? How was it presented? What popular impact did it have?

Para 2. What image did Hitler convey? Why was this attractive?

Para 3. In what ways did the Nazi party attract popular support? Why was this? What impression did it give?

Para 4. What policies did the Nazis present? Why did they gain support? What did they offer which was new.

Para 5. How far did economic circumstances and disappointment with Versailles affect Nazi popularity?

Having seen how analysis can help dismantle a question and construct an argument, you may try the process on one or two of the following examples:

THE RISE OF HITLER AND THE NAZIS

1. *'If the army had not stood on our side, we should not be standing here today.' (Adolf Hitler 1933). What was the significance of the army in securing and consolidating Hitler's power before 1931?*

2. *Comment on the view that without the economic difficulties experienced by Germany before 1933, the Nazis would not have come to power.*

3. *Examine Hitler's personal contribution to the popular success of the Nazi party in 1935.*

MUSSOLINI

1. *Assess Mussolini's domestic policies and achievements to 1935.*

2. *How important was fear of the Socialists in bringing Mussolini to power?*

3. *Examine the results of the Abyssinian War for Italy and Europe.*

FROM QUESTION ANALYSIS TO PARAGRAPH HEADINGS:

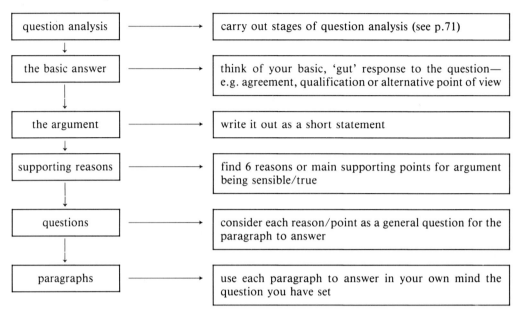

question analysis	carry out stages of question analysis (see p.71)
the basic answer	think of your basic, 'gut' response to the question— e.g. agreement, qualification or alternative point of view
the argument	write it out as a short statement
supporting reasons	find 6 reasons or main supporting points for argument being sensible/true
questions	consider each reason/point as a general question for the paragraph to answer
paragraphs	use each paragraph to answer in your own mind the question you have set

I. CHECKLIST

1. Your ability to use your knowledge to answer a specific question is crucial.

2. Questions are designed to reflect the unique interests and problems of History.

3. Most questions are of a type which require some assessment and/or explanation.

4. Questions can be broken down into their component parts.

5. Paraphrasing the question brings its key factor, phrase or word to the fore.

6. Questions will tell you about themselves and their implications.

7. Look for the parts and whole of a topic and the relative importance of the parts.

8. Be historical and realistic in your assessment of success, failure or achievement.

9. Patience and analysis will make difficult questions or quotations understandable.

10. Define unusual or key words.

11. Try to develop a critical frame of mind in all historical work.

12. Reduce and contain your answer to start with:
    (a) seek an argument.
    (b) find the reasons to support it.

13. Consider your reasons as posing a question for each paragraph.

ESSAY WRITING

About this Chapter

This chapter will explain the importance of logical structure, argument and relevance in essay writing. It views writing essays not as a series of isolated events but as the dynamic process of developing a skill. The work suggested here is to enhance the writer's awareness and promote discussion. Class or non-examination essays are the main concern of the chapter.

The purpose of the previous chapters has been to help you have the right preparation. If you have followed the advice and tried the exercises you will understand a little better the basic skills of studying History. Careful reading and thoughtful, precise note making are essential to good essay writing.

A. UNDERSTANDING THE ESSAY

The Purpose of the Essay

The reason for writing history essays is not that your teacher has given you a deadline and you are running out of excuses. Although this may be a powerful motive, it is not the best reason. The essay has a vital part to play in historical study as an important way for the historian to demonstrate his reading and thinking.

Essays will be a central part of your work, both during the course and finally in examinations where you will need to use them to demonstrate historical knowledge, skills and thought.

To see what is required in an Advanced Examination look back to p.65 ('The Purpose of Questions'). Your essays are answers which try to satisfy these requirements.

> The History essay is a logical argument in words which demonstrates historical knowledge, skills and understanding.

Approaches to Essay Writing

TYPE	METHOD	REASONS FOR METHOD	ADVANTAGES OF METHOD	DISADVANTAGES OF METHOD
'Sit down and do it'	Writes essay straight off, without planning or preparing from notes, old essays, text books, memory. 'that will do.' 'I must get it done for tomorrow.'	1. Laziness. 2. Disorganisation. 3. Incompetence. 4. Carelessness/ casualness. 5. Lack of time. 6. Brilliance.	1. Quick. 2. Meets deadlines. 3. Leaves time for football, discos, T.V.	1. Inadequate time for thinking. 2. Rough or poor appearance. 3. Imperfect expression of ideas. 4. Irrelevance. 5. Disjointed.
'Planning'	Plans essay and resources to be used, then writes up.	1. Has read 'The Modern History Manual' 2. Good organisation of time. 3. Efficient.	1. Efficient use of time. 2. Considered, relevant essay. 3. Logical arrangement of ideas and materials 4. Excellent preparation for examinations.	
'In rough, then in neat'	Writes out whole essay in rough form, copies up into a neat version.	1. Misguided concern for appearance above relevance, argument and general content. 2. Masochism. 3. Concern to produce a definitive essay; a contribution to the wisdom of the ages.	1. Neat final essay. 2. Well constructed relevant essay? 3. Better than those following the 'sit down and do it' approach.	1. Uses vast amounts of time—very slow. 2. Essays can become shorter in length, therefore inadequate treatment of question. 3. Tendency to copy out plans in fuller form during exams.

'Sit down and do it—the inspired approach?!'

The Essay as Practice

You may recognise your own approach to essay writing in the table showing three approaches to the problem. Of course, these approaches are not exclusive; many students will combine or vary them. You may consider presenting the first draft, if it is not too messy, but be prepared to copy it out again if it is not acceptable.

We seem to have been harsh in criticising the 'in rough then neat' writers. You may think that it is good to produce a neat, legible and carefully presented essay. Indeed it is. To have pride in the appearance of the final product is commendable. For those whose rough copy is very rough it may be essential to produce a 'good' copy! But many of those people who spend time making a good copy need not do so if they thought about the essay properly beforehand. What is more, there are hidden dangers in following the 'in rough then neat' approach.

In order to appreciate those hidden dangers we should understand the place of an essay in the two years of an A level History course. Two years have been set aside to allow time to study a period of History in sufficient depth. It is also time to perfect the skills of the historian. To develop the skill of writing a polished, precise and mature essay can take between two years and a lifetime. The important thing is the skill or technique of essay writing itself. Any one essay is merely evidence of the degree of skill or technique which has been achieved.

Looking at it another way, imagine that you have been asked to make a bookcase in a craft lesson. The important thing about the task is the skill of making joints, which is gained in this case from making a bookcase. Even if the bookcase falls down or breaks, the skill of joining pieces of wood has been practised and will remain with the student and be practised in other ways. The bookcase may be useful as a bookcase just as the essay once written may contain useful understanding and knowledge. However, the finished product is really expendable, once the lesson has been learned from it and the teacher's comment understood. The mistake that many students make is to consider the product, in this case an A level essay, more important in itself than the process which produced it. Those who write 'in rough and then in neat' make this mistake. *Essays are consumable at A level—use them to feed the skill of writing History*. For most students the only essays which really count are the ones they will write in the final examination. As you will not see the titles before the examination, it is better to take the skill of essay writing with you into the examination room, than memorised chunks of your old essays. They will not be enough on their own, nor is it likely that you will be able to make them fit the question set.

Were it possible to take a pill after which the most perfect essays flowed from your pen, A level History courses would be completed more rapidly. Sadly this is not the case. You have been given two years not only to investigate historical thinking and knowledge but also to practise the dynamic process of essay writing. Do not see each essay as an isolated event. It is a marker point in the course of learning to write history essays. Be patient. Do not worry about bad marks—you can learn from them. Each time reconsider how you prepare and write essays. Your teacher's comments on the essay will help improve your knowledge and understanding. Do not resent the number of essays you have to write, as the old saying goes 'practice makes perfect'!

> 'Other candidates tend to write out a plan which is lengthy in the extreme, only to write out in sentence form the plan as an answer.'
> (J.M.B. Examiners' Report:
> A level History, 1982, p.35)

'Essays are consumable at A level. Use them to feed the skill of writing.'

B. BEFORE YOU START

Starting the Essay: The Plan

Faced with a few books, a folder of notes and a title, how do you start to write a history essay? The simple answer, *if all your preparations are complete*, is just start! But you should begin a history essay long before you are faced with actually writing it. You should start as the planners do; draw up a plan or outline for the essay in some form. Even those students intending to make a good copy of their rough essay may plan their writing. The detail and type of plan used will vary considerably from student to student. For some

the plan will be a series of single words or phrases which will act as the key to each paragraph, giving either the subject, idea, or argument for the paragraph. Frequently the plan of a few words may be the first thing that comes into a student's head or more ominously the only thing in the student's head! At the other extreme are those planners who compose the most thorough set of notes for their essays. They will just stop short of putting the essential pieces of knowledge, understanding and argument into good English. The amount of detail in a plan is something that will vary with circumstances and a student's knowledge. One thing is definite. *A plan is essential for good essay writing.*

Let us see some plans and how they can help.

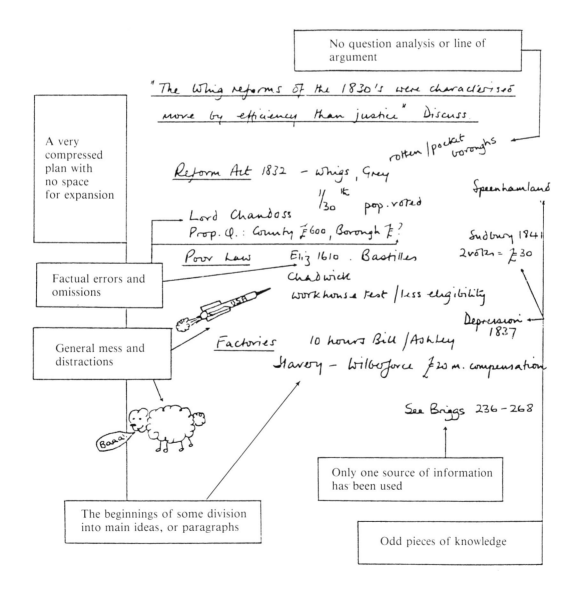

WHY IS A PLAN SO IMPORTANT?

1. The argument of your essay takes its unique shape in the plan. (Remember, as we have seen, an essay is a logical argument in words.)

2. Your argument is tested in the plan to see if it is convincing.

3. All your resources—thinking and information, are brought together in the plan.

4. You see if you have enough information to answer the essay in the plan. Your resources confront the essay title.

5. Your plan gives an outline shape to the essay in paragraphs or chunks of connected information and ideas.

6. The plan prevents mistakes, waffle, inaccuracy and repetition.

7. The plan makes writing the essay quicker.

It (a) allows you to concentrate on expressing your ideas,
  (b) helps you keep your place in an essay, because you can see what you have written and what comes next.

8. If you are used to planning, you will produce a more relevant and direct answer in examinations. (Examination plans tend to be briefer but the mental training in ordinary essays is important.)

The weaknesses of this plan are pointed out. A plan must begin with an understanding of the question. This is achieved by question analysis, which is neglected here. The writer has used the plan as an aid to memory, jotting down, in a haphazard fashion, things that come to mind or seem useful. This may be of some value, but the plan should be made to work harder.

HOW TO PLAN FOR ESSAYS	REASONS
1. Use plenty of space.	It will be easier to read and follow when writing.
2. Plan in pencil with a rubber.	It will allow you to re-arrange and correct information.
3. Leave a margin.	Still more notes may be added as you write.
4. Analyse the question parts.	This leads to a line of argument.
5. State the line of argument.	This gives overall direction to the essay and helps the introduction.
6. Separate out main ideas or areas of knowledge and make them your subheadings.	Each may then take a paragraph in your final essay.
7. Fill in the facts, quotations, comments, thoughts which fit these subheadings.	These will form the main body of your essay.
8. Keep your notes near at hand.	You will need to search your notes for the details and materials you need.
9. Use reference and text books.	(a) To check your notes. (b) To search out extra information.

EXERCISE

You can use the next plan to see how all this advice has been followed. Look at some of your plans for essays. How do they compare?

"The Whig reforms of the 1830's were characterised more by efficiency than justice" Discuss

Line of argument

> efficiency characterised manner + products of reform — 'justice' inspired some reform — error to measure C19th by standards of C20th.

Intro : important foundations for future — Benthamite utilitarian influence strong, justice / humanitarian influence. Reform act = efficiency in social order. manner motive / argument : reality / effect.   Chadwick

Para 1   Reform Act :- limited, partial, moderate ; seen as revol. (168 seats to go)
:- 'justice' the unrepresented cities (160000 / 16m voters)
:- small extension to M/class ∴ support system makes econ. power. Injustice cont. — Chartism
:- fears for legis. intro. by reformed House **but** all based on efficiency   ACCL
:- elections simpler, cheaper, uniform ∴ efficient? b**ut** corruption

Para 2   New P.L. 1834   "emperor + duke of Somerset House"
:- util. / Chadwick / w/H. test + less elig. pure Bentham
:- results o/door relief cont., fall in cost (£6¾ m 1830/4 : ↓ 4½ 1835-9)   "1st gt. piece of legis. based on scientific or econ. principles"
:- no justice for mass of labour.   Chadwick
:- relationship P.L. — labour mkt., needs for act of lab.
    nb: method: inspect, report, legis, monitor

Para 3   Factory Reform
:- Ashley 10/hours — justice
:- cotton mills : Act daylight / relay / no educ.   U13 48hrs no U9
:- cf Wilberforce Slavery, motives, effect.

Para 4   Municipal Corp. Act.

The Introduction

Every essay will contain an introduction, a middle and a conclusion. The middle as we have seen will be an argument, discussion or series of reasoned points in answer to the question set. When students ask 'how do you start an essay?' they usually mean what should they write for a first sentence. It is the first sentence which is so hard to compose. The second sentence may be a little easier and usually by the end of the first paragraph, students feel more secure; they are 'into' the essay.

In a desire to get something down on paper quickly the student is underestimating the power and importance of the introduction. The introduction is in many ways the most important part of the essay.

Here is an example of an introduction which was written in a rush to get something down on paper.

'How much truth is there in the view that while Gladstone's first ministry was outstanding, his second was a disaster?'

'W. E. Gladstone (1809–98) was one of England's greatest statesmen, who enjoyed two major periods of office, 1868–74 and 1880–85. Gladstone saw most political questions as involving morality in some form or another. Gladstone was dogged by the problems of Ireland to which his sense of duty drew him. Foreign affairs were a cause of much criticism for Gladstone and the Liberals particularly over the Sudan. His governments were responsible for some major pieces of social legislation, for example in education, bureaucracy (1870), Trade Unions (1871), the law and electoral reform.'

Even though the writer may have planned out the essay and a line of argument, this is not a very successful beginning. It is too concerned with fact and makes little reference to the question. The factual information may have a place later on in the essay but as it is used here, as an introduction, it does not do a useful job.

What is the job of the introduction? Very simply, it introduces the essay or *argument*. It prepares the way for the main body of the essay or answer to the question and should do more than just 'set the scene'. The introduction should be a *statement of intent*. It is important for the writer because it lays out a line of attack along which the essay will proceed. You may like to think of the essay as a journey; in the introduction you give the directions and the likely route that will be taken. You may even wish to say what things of interest may be seen along that route.

As the introduction says how you intend to proceed, you are committing yourself to a particular course. If you change course later on in the essay, it will be obvious that you do not know where you are going or that you have not planned your essay with enough care.

> 'All candidates should be made aware of the crucial importance of the introductory sentences, possibly extending to a short paragraph to each answer they produce. This is the initial action, the first step, and, for the writer, it can determine the whole nature of the response that will be made because it imposes, almost unconsciously, a straight-jacket on the thought, development and structure that will thereafter be pursued.'
> (J.M.B. Examiners' Report:
> A level History, 1979, p.18)

As well as influencing the writer, the introduction has a profound effect on the reader. Everyone forms some sort of impression of a person the first time that they meet. So it is with an essay. The first thing that a reader meets is the introduction.

WHAT THE INTRODUCTION SHOULD GIVE THE READER

Parts of the introduction	Functions of parts
1. An assessment of the topic.	Should show that the writer (a) has understood the general area or topic for discussion and (b) has a good grasp of the relevant information.
2. Line of argument, important theme or idea.	Should outline how the writer intends to proceed because (a) this is the main function of the introduction and (b) it proves that the specific question has been understood.
3. Transition to start of argument.	Should allow smooth movement to the first paragraph of the essay.

Your most startling, persuasive or important points should not go in the introduction; do not let the introduction steal your thunder. If you can satisfy these three requirements the reader should gain a good first impression of both the essay and the writer. In this way you should hold the reader's attention.

What is more, if the introduction is clear, precise, forthright, logical and interesting the reader will remember that initial impression and perhaps forgive any purple or turgid passages which may follow! It is well known that we remember best what comes first and what comes last in any period of study or reading. This is known as 'primacy' and 'recency' of memory. This should make us take extra care with introductions and conclusions. They will be the parts of the essay most likely to be remembered in any general impression.

> 'The introductory sentences are crucial, too, in that they can mould and determine the reader's reception of an answer. Whereas the good introduction impresses, the poor one depresses, conditioning the reader to anticipate inaccuracy, poor understanding, irrelevancy, muddled thinking—all the qualities, in fact, which the experienced examiner has come to associate with the weak or poor response.'
> (J.M.B. Examiners' report: A level History, 1979, p.19)

C. THE MECHANICS OF ESSAY WRITING: PARTS AND SKILLS

Writing an Introduction

As we have said, it takes much practice to be able to write essays well. In order to get those all important first sentences right, you can practise writing to a pattern. This is not meant to be the only way of constructing your opening paragraph. It is merely a device or method to get you started. Treat it as an exercise. It should help! When you feel more confident and are more experienced you can dispense with the method.

THE INTRODUCTION NEEDS:

(a) an *assessment* of the topic	2 sentences
(b) line of *argument*, important theme or idea	2 sentences
(c) *transition* to start of argument, evidence or main body of the essay	2 sentences
Total:	6 sentences

The total of six sentences is an arbitrary figure, but many students have found it useful as a guideline. You can vary the pattern according to the question, your knowledge or understanding. When time is important, as in examinations, it can make sense to reduce the number of sentences.

> 'Many candidates . . . write long introductions packed with unnecessary detail or fail to 'introduce' their essays with perceptive comment which gives direction to their answers.'
> (J.M.B. Examiners' Report: A level History, 1982, p.44)

Reconsider this planned essay with the introduction broken down into the parts as suggested.

'The Whig reforms of the 1830's were characterised more by efficiency than justice.' Discuss.

(a) ASSESSMENT—general comment, identifying major reforms under discussion.	The reforms of the 1830's laid important foundations for the future. Beginning with the Parliamentary Reform of 1832, the Whig ministry proceeded to reform the legislation concerning the Poor Laws 1834, Factories and local government 1835. (2 sentences)

(b) ARGUMENT—main points mentioned:
  (i) efficiency predominated
  (ii) justice depends on points of view.
	There was a strong emphasis on efficiency based on the ideas of Jeremy Bentham and utilitarianism in all this legislation. Though the voice of humanitarians and evangelists was heard. What was 'just' for the wealthy powerful minority was often unjust for the majority of the nation.
	(3 sentences)

(c) TRANSITION—intention to proceed by looking at the Reform Act.	Consideration of the Great Reform Act will show that the use of 20th Century democratic ideals and hindsight can distort our view of the justice of the measure. One real concern of reformers was to prevent social disorder disrupting the efficient working of the country. (2 sentences)

Let us see how the mediocrity of an earlier example has been overcome using this method.

'How much truth is there in the view that while Gladstone's first ministry was outstanding, his second was a disaster?'

(a) ASSESSMENT—general observations about the two periods.	Between 1868 and 1874 Gladstone pursued a courageous and energetic campaign which reformed the State. This was achieved often at the expense of those whom Gladstone's political intuition told him were the natural leaders of the nation; his second ministry (1880–84) was barren by comparison.
(b) ARGUMENT—direct dealing with the terms of the question.	Some historians have criticised Gladstone's earlier period of office for reforming institutions rather than society. Such a criticism it will be argued, is unjustified. Certainly Gladstone's view of society was less useful in 1880 when he returned to power for a second time, then, as Chamberlain reminded him, social legislation had become a parliamentary issue.
(c) TRANSITION—intention to proceed with the outstanding first ministry.	The failure of Gladstone's second ministry is partly due to the Disraelian legacy, and partly a result of Gladstone's reaction to the new political circumstances of his return. During the first ministry changes for example in the army, universities and Civil Service were revolutionary.

EXERCISE

Take one of your recent essays and rewrite the introduction according to the pattern suggested. Use the comments of your teacher and any discussion of the essay. Begin by carefully analysing the question.

Structuring the Essay

A serious difficulty encountered by many students when writing an essay is organising the information. At the start, the composition of an essay seems a dauntingly endless task. The activity of question analysis and planning should ease the burden and reduce the mystery of essay writing.

For further help set a limit to the number of paragraphs you will use.

e.g. USE THE SIX PARAGRAPH RULE, because:

1. It is an arbitrary figure but certain students find it helpful.
2. It contains the problem, limits the essay.
3. It allows you to work within those paragraphs to achieve the best effect.
4. You control the essay, the essay does not control you.
5. Paragraphs have to have a purpose. They start when you wish.
6. It forces you to think concisely and answer efficiently.

If your knowledge and answer demands the use of seven or eight paragraphs, use them. So long as you set a limit to the essay you will have confidence and control. No longer will you find yourself pushing on to a point where you say 'that will do' and hastily include a few rounding off sentences. We used six points or ideas in Question Analysis. This is where your six paragraphs will probably come from.

A NOTE FORM ESSAY ON THE SPANISH CIVIL WAR.

Title	Account for the outbreak of the Civil War in Spain.
Question Analysis	See Question Analysis chapter.
Line of Argument	Structural/institutional: failure of trad. institutions, e.g. Church, army, monarchy, Republic to come to terms with econ. change of C20th.
Para 1	*Social/econ. context* Pop. growth (1900 18.5 m: 1936 25 m) low level ind. (pa income p.head ½ average Ind. europ.) Sp. declines no ind. revol. nor Mid/class to stabilise, reduce polarisation — 2 nations ∴ work/cl. = large, low std. of liv., illiteracy (25%, 1936). Stagnant econ. Medieval Agric. (2m landowners 44% land/4m peasants, 1929). Inflation + depress. hit. Sp. 1920's/30's (Wall St Crash = Sp trade 1933 = ½ 1929) These econ/social condits. prod political pressures + conflict.
Para 2	*Political pressures* Violence = feature of Sp. pol. life (1808-1936 = 4 civil wars, 13 part ch. of constit., 109 successive govts., 40 pronunciamentos) Trad. pol. syst. reflected econ. divisions. Monarch + feudal squirearchy, heirs to empire kept a brake on change (ind. + pol) aided by forces of conserv.ism/reaction = army + church. Prod. of pol. inertia = radical ideas + feelings flourished Anarch + Comm. pop, with masses (Anarch = 1.5 m, 1933; led Oliver + Pestana, less scrupulous — Durruti) Vigorous Trade Unism. = evidence pop. oppos. to state = Socialist UGT + anarch CNT. Pol/econ divisions mirrored in competition of centre/region = wealthy, ind. Basq + Catalan provinces (N.) pulled hard vs. Castilian centralist yoke, anxious to enjoy polit. indep. they could afford.
Para 3	The failure of constitutional govt. birth of republic 1930 Primo de Rivera's 'brief parenthesis' (since 1923) in constit. govt. ended = Dictatorship success due 1) luck 2) world econ. upturn. Opposit. cont. because fail to generate new instit. (e.g. new polit. party, Nat. assembly) + old ones fail to evolve to solve Sp. econ/soc. problems. Unity of oppositions (Zamora, Azana, Cabellero -UGT), lid off after Primo 12.4.1931 Monarchy removed (14th, Alfonso XIII abdicates = 1st institution to go) Sp. without a general will, next as old as monarchy — church disunity, royalists, RCs, business.
Para 4	*Destruction of the Middle ground/Rapid polarisation of sides*. Ch. = nat. target for Libs. May 1931, June 28th election massive turnout = triumph for Left. Cortes = variety "there are 473 parties in the Cortes". No consensus to replace instits., Repub. attacked. Moves vs. Ch. = unwise (20% Sp. = RC) Culturally/Spiritually embedded in Sp. Constit. separation Ch/state nationalise Ch. prop., secularizing educ. + 1932 dissol. of Jesuits alienated part of Sp. soc. esp. the centre. Note 1933 elections Religion: large no. of women vote for 1st time. Old Instit: army (reduced 16-8 divs, 22k-105k men) failure on land reform, nationalise pub. service inds all contrib. to deteriorating econ. Azana's capitulation to demands for Catalan indep. 1931 (flag, president + Parliament) divide Sp. further + more calls for autonomy. Lack of middle ground/polarisation shown by Para 5, 6. →
Para 5	*Revival of the Rt. Nov–Feb 1933* aim: destroy Lib. repub. work, army important role, violent period (Dec. 1933 Anarch. in Barcelona, Catalan indept. declared Oct. 1934, Asturian Commune — brutally crushed 3,000 d. 70K wounded, Franco/Sp. N.Afri. units).
Para 6	*Popular Front 1936* PF + alliance of Left. "those who preferred Moscow to Sp". (Robles) Victorious, amnesty, (Syndicalists, Comm. Reps., Socialists, Anarch.) vs. broad Rt. (Monarch, Conserv., etc.) squeezed out centre of Sp. pol. L278 C56 R137. Polarisation May '36 Zamora out, Azana in as Pres. power = Lt. monopoly. Anarchy + collective violence "everything and at once". PF attacks Sp. institutions, anti-clerical., estates seized by peasants, strikes, massive unrest, Polarising shown by violence of Falangists/Anarch. extremists. UGT 'encourage' Repub. by strikes. 16th Feb–15th June 1936, 160 ch. burned, 269 assass., 1287 wounded, 146 buildings, 113 strikes. Lightning strikes early July = paralysis (800,000 involved). For Rt. Fascism = only answer to Anarch + Comm. Revol. Army contemplate coup, quiet under Lerroux govt. Soleto's murder (July '36) = opportunity, save fatherland, restore order, failed (all army didn't follow Franco, Mola + Sanjurjo 18th July '36, Alzamiento) Anarch/Social militia rally to govt. — war.
Conclusion	Sp C/W — context of Sp. Soc./econ/soc stresses of 20's/30's Repub. — no power base, M/C, bureaucracy, stabilise attack on institutions, undermine consensus, polit. vacuum minority of Repub., no evolved replacements. Repub. failed materially improve maj. of Sp. people lost faith. Radical solutions — war.

Selecting the Information

Remind yourself of the objectives of the examination questions (p.65). The writer of the previous essay plan has demonstrated advanced skills by *selecting* the information or facts *relevant* to the question and presenting it in *a logical argument*. These skills are fundamental to writing a good historical essay and will be discussed in the next three sections.

When writing a history essay, most people have more *facts* or knowledge available than they can conveniently use. If you have twenty pages of notes, it is obvious that not all of those twenty pages can go into your essay! The simple answer is that you must select information from your notes to suit the question. This may appear obvious but it is surprising how many essays are spoiled because students include too much information—more particularly, information which is not relevant or does not suit their argument. Sometimes students repeat facts or information in a slightly different way. Piling up information for the sake of it can reveal a lack of understanding. In short, what you leave out of an essay can be as important as what you put in! Remember that it is better to kill the reader with kindness by selecting information for him than to batter him to death in a flurry of factual blows!

To think of it another way, if you were asked to mend a broken chair you would not use every tool you had just for the sake of showing that you had them. So it is with information and the essay. You only need to use the information that is suitable or relevant to that particular essay. Some pieces of information must go unused despite the fact that you have them available. Do not be lazy or shy about information; exploit your notes. Their value is determined by your particular purpose or essay. Be ruthless with your notes. Vigorously re-organise and select the information for the best effect and to suit your planned answer.

EXERCISE

The following pieces of information are taken from the student's notes on the Spanish Civil War and are in no particular order. None of these notes have been directly used in the essay plan (p.92). Read them through carefully. Consider each piece of information in turn. Would you have *selected* any of these pieces of information to go in the essay? Where would they fit? Why would you wish to include them? How far do they develop, repeat or support a point? What is the significance of each item? Which notes would not be useful for the essay? What are the connections between the pieces of information? Can they be grouped together under titles? Ask your teacher's advice.

1. Accion Popular = clerical party, basis of Rt., clashed with Repub. led by Herrera (ed. of El debate/future cardinal) defeated 1931 gave way to CEDA led by neo nazi Robles.

2. "Africa begins at the Pyrenees".

3. 1900 Peasantry = 69% of population 1929 Census showed 50,000 registered beggars.

4. Anarchists rejected govt. and state, fought with equal determination against supporters of Robles, socialists of Caballero and communists of Diaz.

5. Army trad. more involved in politics in Sp. than other European countries. General Mola sacked as Chief of staff (March 1936), Franco dismissed as Governor of Canary Islands (March 1936).

6. No evidence that Italy or Germany had prior knowledge of outbreak of war yet arms + aircraft sent within a fortnight of rising 15th July 1936.

7. Repub. dissolved the ancient Military orders whose origins lay in the Reconquest.

8. Spain geog. isolation, acidic soil, harsh climate.

EXAMPLE:
PART OF A STUDENT'S ANSWER

Account for the outbreak of civil war in Spain

Note 1. Useful detail supporting diversity of political opinion in Cortes on the losing side in the 1931 election. Contrast with note 4.

Note 3. Supporting detail of economy of Spain, matched with note 8. 1900 figure not as pertinent as 1929 census.

Relevance

Having agreed that some form of selection must take place, how do we go about selecting? The inclusion or exclusion of information is decided by our historical experience which is gained by reading, discussion and thought. The more you practise the better you will become at selecting historical information to suit firstly your essay and secondly your argument.

One thing you will have noticed if you were discussing the selection of the pieces of information on the Spanish Civil War is the need to justify your choices or decisions. You cannot reject a piece of information without giving an explanation. The reasons why you include something will be decided by your understanding, your question analysis and your line of argument.

In the main, selecting information occurs at the question analysis and planning stages of writing. To help decide on the relevance of a piece of information you can ask questions of it as suggested in Question Analysis.

Understanding the relevance of a piece of information is really assessing how *important* it is; it depends on what you are writing whether a piece of information is useful or relevant.

In 1832 after much agitation, the Whig Reform Bill became law. This chart shows how a fact may be used in a variety of ways according to the historian's purpose.

'A plan is essential for good essay writing'

SOME POSSIBLE USES OF A SIMPLE FACT.

Use	Source	Example
Medical History	W. E. B. Lloyd, 'A Hundred Years of Medicine'. (London 2nd ed., 1968) p.248)	'The Great Reform Bill of 1832 may be fairly called the beginning of public health legislation'
Political thought	J. Plamenatz, 'Man and Society, Vol 2.' (London, 1963) p. 94	'. . . the July Revolution in France and the passage of the first Reform Bill in England, two events which aroused great hopes among the poor and led to great disappointments'.
Urban History	A. Briggs, 'Victorian Cities' (Harmondsworth, 1968) p.90	'. . . in the course of the Reform Bill struggles of the years 1831 and 1832 Manchester enhanced its reputation as a centre of social disturbances, even as a possible cradle of revolution'.
Trade Union History	A. E. Masson, 'British Trade Unions 1800–1875.' (London, 1972) p.40	'. . . disillusionment with the Reform Bill may have combined with trade recovery to stimulate Trade Unionism in 1833-34 . . .'
Biography	J. Clive, 'Macauley,' (New York, 1973) p.140	'Macauley's great reputation as a parliamentary orator derived from the part he played in the Reform Bill debates'.
Political History	G. Kitson Clark 'The Making of Victorian England.' (London, 1962) p.5	'Nor have the writers of textbooks, nor I am afraid many of the teachers in schools, abandoned that curious legend that the middle class came to dominate politics and the country immediately after the Reform Bill of 1832'.

In the same way pieces of information may be used in an essay or several essays. However, the point or purpose of using the same fact will be different depending on the title or direction of the essay.

The vital thing to do is to make sure that the reader understands *why* you are including a particular piece of information. Here we are dealing with the difference between *implicit and explicit relevance*. The relevance is implicit when it is left to the reader to appreciate the importance of a point within that particular answer. Explicit relevance is where the writer plainly states the importance of a point in relation to the question being dealt with. When students fail to make explicit the relevance of a piece of information, they are usually seen as not understanding or merely relying on memory.

AN EXAMPLE OF HOW TO CREATE EXPLICIT RELEVANCE:

On 4th June 1832 after much agitation, debate and difficulty the Reform Bill became law. After separate Bills for Scotland and Ireland the total electorate of the United Kingdom rose from 478,000 to 814,000. } IMPLICIT

On its own the reader may be justified in thinking of this extract, 'so what?'. The relevance of these facts must be clearly or explicitly stated if they are used in an essay. Take the first sentence only of the implicit example,

On 4th June 1832 after much agitation, debate and difficulty the Reform Bill became law; *that this happened peacefully without revolution or dictatorship was a major achievement.* } EXPLICIT

Here the significance of the fact for the development of democratic government is made. We could draw the reader's attention to other points.

On 4th June 1832 after much agitation, debate and difficulty the Reform Bill became law. After separate Bills for Scotland and Ireland, the total electorate for the United Kingdom rose from 478,000 to 814,000. *Although the immediate effects were small, the ultimate consequences were immense: Through the door which the Reform Act opened came important social and administrative reforms.* ⎱ EXPLICIT

Explain clearly why you have included pieces of information. Make their relevance to your essay title or line of argument obvious. Reconsider, at various points in the essay, both the implications of the title and the actual wording of it. This should prevent wandering and waffle in your answer. Never assume the reader will know what you are referring to. The reader needs to be guided through the information you have selected.

It is interesting to see a professional historian reminding the reader *explicitly* of the relevance of his facts, analysis and discussion. In Chapter 3 of Henry Pelling's book 'Popular Politics and Society in Late Victorian Britain' (2nd edition London 1979) the author examines some of the problems of using the concept of a 'Labour aristocracy'. Pelling's central idea is that the value of this concept is variable and its use needs care. In Pelling's contribution to the Labour aristocracy debate the reader is reminded explicitly of the author's position by comments like:

1. "Only in the 1840's and later did the situation begin to improve markedly; and the class which now emerged into comparative prosperity was not an élite of labour aristocrats but a more homogenous class of factory workers..." (p.47)

2. "Employment on the railways as in other sections of the transport industry cannot be said to have been of such a character as to fit in with the theory of labour aristocracy." (p.51)

3. "There was no real labour aristocracy in the staple export trades — coal and the main branches of textile manufacture". (p.52)

4. "The concept of the Labour aristocracy has had its value in drawing attention to differences within the working class but if it implies the existence... of a labour élite distinctly separated from lower strata and marked by political behaviour of an acquiesent type then it is a concept that does more harm than good to historical truth". (p.61)

EXERCISE

Explain the relevance of the pieces of information below for each of the essay titles which follow. The relevance or 'usefulness' will vary for each piece of information in relation to each title. Say how each might or might not 'fit in'. Check your notes to explain the information, seek the advice of your teacher.

INFORMATION

1. Helmult von Moltke was appointed Chief of the Prussian General staff in 1857.

2. In 1834 the Zollverein (Maassen) came into existence, by 1836 it included 25 states and 26 million inhabitants.

3. "Politics is not in itself an exact and logical science but it is the capacity to choose in each fleeing moment of the situation that which is least harmful or most opportune."

4. In Prussia the Catholic Centre party saw the state as protective of the Citizens' rights, should concern itself with the social conditions of the less well off, stood for freedom or religious rights.

5. Whilst disliking the British 'model' of Government which reduced monarchical power. Bismarck insisted on universal manhood suffrage for the Reichstag.

ESSAYS

(A) Consider the view that diplomacy was more important than warfare in securing the unification of Germany by 1871.

(B) How much credit should be given to Bismarck for the united Germany of 1871?

(C) Examine the problems facing Bismarck in Germany between 1871 and 1890. With what success did he deal with them?

EXAMPLE:
PART OF A STUDENT'S ANSWER

This fact would be useful for Essay A as Moltke was responsible for the military brilliance of the Prussians in the period and with Room for the restructuring of the army, which crisis also brought Bismarck to power on 23rd September 1862. In Essay B this fact might be incorporated in argument to show the other factors which made for unification i.e. the power of the army, the Zollverein and economic prosperity etc. Moltke could be the military opportunist and strategist as could Bismarck! I would be unlikely to use this for Essay C — an example of the military caste?

Logical Argument

As well as selecting the relevant information you must arrange it in a logical way. The most important thing to remember is that every idea, comment or observation must be supported by facts or reasons. It is easy to have an opinion about a moral issue like capital punishment, but if you were to discuss it in an essay you would usually have to give your reasons. So it is with history essays—you can have an opinion but you must back it up with fact or reasons. In historical writing you may need a great deal of factual information to support your argument or opinion.

Use the pattern of statement and supporting reasons or evidence when writing.

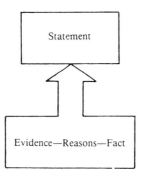

We can observe historians using this method.

1. STATEMENT	A major obstacle to the development of a formal education for middle- and upper-class girls was the general view that moral superiority in the female was balanced by a corresponding intellectual infirmity.'
SUPPORTING EVIDENCE FOR STATEMENT ABOUT THE COMMONLY HELD VIEW IN THE 19th CENTURY THAT WOMEN WERE INTELLECTUALLY FRAIL	Progressives argued that this was the result of girls receiving an inferior education, and authoritative support for this view was given by the Taunton Commission in 1868 (120) . . . Conservative social attitudes were buttressed by physiological work on the brain, which indicated that a woman's brain weighed five ounces less than that of a man. When the finding was related to Darwinistic thinking it seemed obvious that as G. J. Romanes wrote in 1887 ''it must take many centuries for heredity to produce the necessary five ounces of the female brain'' (122)' Anne Digby and P. Searby, *Children, School and Society in the 19th Century England.* (London, 1981) p.49

Notice in the last example the scholarly device of numbered notes is used. An historical fact may be proven or confirmed by reference to evidence. Historians use notes principally to tell people where their facts and evidence come from. Another historian or student may wish to check the evidence. It is much the same with scientists who give details of the experiments they used to obtain their results. Another scientist can repeat the experiments to check the results and see if the conclusions are true. It is not normal for A level students to use footnotes, but it is sensible to know why and how they are used.

2. STATEMENT	'The Irish Government trod its thorny neutral path as delicately as possible and developed a remarkable capacity for not noticing disagreeable facts.'
SUPPORTING EVIDENCE FOR THE STATEMENT ABOUT THE DIFFICULTY OF IRISH NEUTRALITY 1939–45	'Thus on the one hand it turned a blind eye to British aircraft flying over Donegal or the return of stranded British airmen across the border and on the other hand it managed to ignore for a considerable time the existence of a wireless transmitter in the German embassy.' F. S. L. Lyons, *Ireland since the Famine,* (London, 1973) p.556

'Essay writing is not a mechanical process.'

Writing an essay is not a mechanical process. You may adopt the principle of statement and reasons, facts or evidence to your style and purpose. It is possible in a sense to work in 'reverse', giving particular details and drawing a conclusion. Professor John Vincent in a long assessment of Gladstone observes 'He was appalled by frivolity, and frivolity was appalled by him, ... "something in the tone of his voice and his way of coming into the room that is not aristocratic. In short, he is not frivolous enough for me: if he were soaked in boiling water ... I do not suppose a single drop of fun would ooze out (316) " And easy-going men like Clarendon would poke fun at "our Jesuit" and his "benevolent nocturnal rambles" (317)'. Vincent concludes. "Thus before 1859 Gladstone was cut off from wide popularity among the Parliamentary class by stiffness and political isolation ..."
J. Vincent. *The Formation of the British Liberal Party* (Harmondsworth, 1966), p.261.

His general comment or conclusion follows the facts or evidence; he is arguing inductively.

The basic principle of giving reasons and evidence governs the building of a logical argument.

Moving from the paragraph to the whole essay, the same principle of building the total argument applies.

EXAMPLE

Examine critically the achievements of the post-war Labour government in domestic policy.

Question analysis and planning may produce a few ideas. For example in handling the post-war British economy and establishing the welfare state the Labour government had a considerable achievement. You may wish to consider the nature of its nationalisation programme and *critically* examine how radical or socialist it was. Each point made must be supported by fact and in turn generates more questions which may be answered in that paragraph. This is how it would look diagramatically.

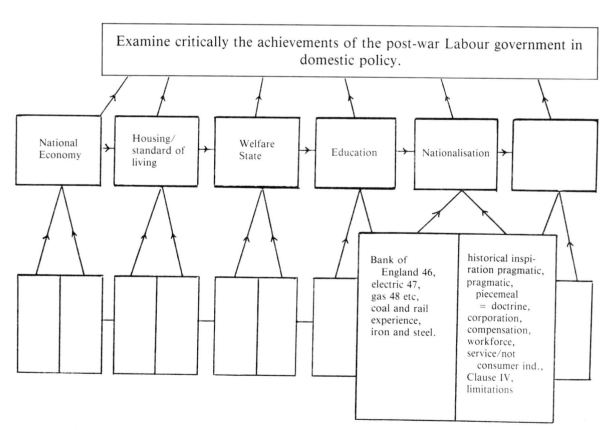

From the diagram we can see how each of the ideas creates a paragraph, which in turn link together to form and answer the question.

OPPOSING VIEWS

Do not worry if the pieces of information or opinions conflict. These opposing views should be brought together in a paragraph or essay. Usually the evidence or argument against your point of view will be presented first.

Do not suppose that all issues are equally balanced. In most cases, historical opinion favours one side or the other. It is the historian's job to do justice to both cases, however strong or weak, and justify his conclusion.

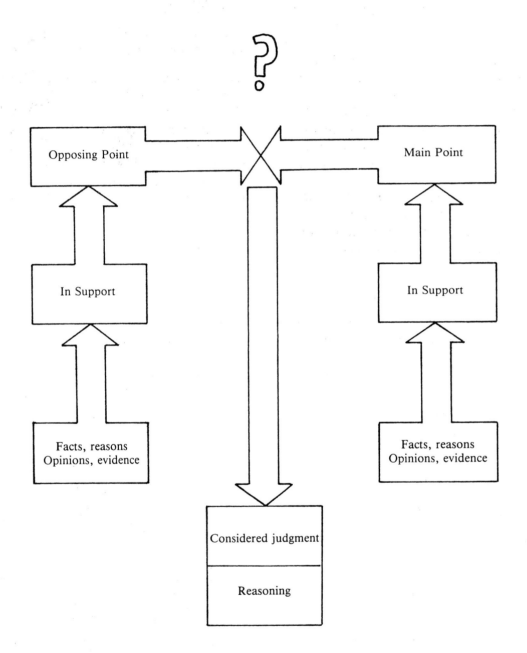

Style

Whilst every student's style of writing will be different, there are some important general points to remember. The style or way of expressing your ideas will create an impression with the reader. Any weaknesses of expression may lead the reader to think that you are weak in understanding, argument or knowledge. *Remember the general A.B.C. when writing: Accuracy, Brevity, Clarity.*

Punctuation

An early problem can occur with students who have little experience of writing essays. It may be a while before they discover the paragraph and then the sentence. Look at this example in answer to the question, ' *"Too little and too late to save Tsarist Russia" Consider this view of the reforms initiated during the reign of Nicholas II'*.

'It's true to say that there was a great deal of discontent in Russia during the reign of Nicholas II, indeed there were things wrong with Russian society that needed reforming badly, whilst the ruling class lived in unabashed luxury the peasants who made up 90 per cent of the population had to be contend with lack of food and primitive living conditions added to this was was a completely ineffective educational system which meant that illiteracy was widespread, thus problems were on a large scale in Russia social reforms were desperately needed, as were political reforms since Russia as an autocratic country suppressed any means of political liberation.'

Notice this is all one sentence presented as a paragraph. It leaves the reader breathless and confused. It is a tragedy of punctuation. The writer has not thought or planned out the ideas or points to be made; the clue of 'was was' and doubt about 'contend' and 'content' point to the speed with which it was written. Although superficial and oversimplified, this piece touches upon important background to the reforms of Nicholas II e.g. the absence of a classless educational system, the failure of Alexander II's modernisation of the agricultural base and liberal programme. These points are lost to the reader in the torrent of words. The way to improve this type of writing is to think and plan more carefully. Then try to think of one thing at a time as you write. If this is done, you will not be afraid of forgetting a piece of information and you can concentrate on presenting the information lucidly. Punctuation should clarify and organise the essay, not be seen as a hindrance or unnecessary.

> 'Too many ill-presented, ill-written and extremely long-winded scripts are seen from candidates who seem to have little idea even of the basics of sentence construction.'
>
> (J.M.B. Examiners' Report: A level History, 1983, p.61)

Spelling

Incorrect spelling is unlikely to lose marks. Once again it is the impression that poor spelling creates which is harmful to the writer. Occasionally incorrect spelling can change the meaning of a sentence. For example, consider the implications of confusing 'accepted' and 'excepted'. The simple answer is to learn from mistakes. Check with a dictionary if you are unsure. Here are some of the commonplace words, which, when misspelt, create a poor impression:

separate	disappear	Bismarck
radical	manoeuvres	Mazzini
bureaucracy	antisemitism	Dreyfus
privilege	belligerence	Disraeli
precedent	guerilla	Hardie
amendment	Parliament	Chamberlain
guarantee	assassination	
	received	

It is always good advice to read widely for the sake of your historical knowledge and understanding but also for the improvement of written English.

> 'Though many (candidates) may have ample material they mar their chances by solecism, malapropisms, dreadful spelling and grammatical errors sometimes so gross as to obscure meaning'.
>
> (J.M.B. Examiners' Report: A level History, 1983, p.61)

Abbreviations

It is a very good practice when writing notes to abbreviate certain words or terms which appear repeatedly. However, when writing essays it is not good style to continue this habit. An essay is a formal piece of writing and no matter how irksome, words must be written in full; Hit. for Hitler, Nap. for Napoleon, Glad. for Gladstone and Br. for Britian should not appear. Beware also of the apostophe which leaps about and can often be found in 'mean't' (sic) meant!

'At Advanced level in History, the ability to write serviceable English is a prerequisite but it is even less frequently attained. To be blunt, a substantial minority of candidates are not fully literate.'

(J.M.B. Examiners' Report:
A level History, 1983, p.61)

Quotations

The use of quotations in essays at Advanced level may cause difficulty. There are two types of source for quotation; they may be either primary or secondary in origin. If we define them simply, primary sources are those written at the time by someone usually connected with the event. Secondary sources are written after the time of the event and are usually based on primary sources. Secondary sources for A level essays will probably be the work of historians.

Quotations may:

1. express neatly and attractively an idea, comment or judgement you wish to make.

2. contain an important statement of intent, fact, motivation, understanding or explanation.

3. develop or cover an idea, argument, controversy or point of view.

4. support or emphasise a particular point you have made.

You should be sure of why you are using quotations; they should not be used to show off your reading or to give the impression of knowing more than you do. Neither should quotations be used to express an opinion and thereby avoid expressing your *own* opinion or using your own words.

There are two important aspects of using quotations in essays. Firstly you must select quotations carefully; they must do a job efficiently. Avoid the temptation to select too much.

The second point to be remembered is that introducing a quotation into your essay needs to be done with care. It is not enough to begin every quotation with 'Taylor says . . . ' or 'Thomson writes . . .' or when memory and initiative fall 'some historians say . . .'.

Notice the differing styles of these two writers:

(a) 'The difficulties of restoring the British economy after the war were increased by the Versailles settlement. As Keynes wrote "The Treaty includes no provision for the economic rehabilitation of Europe, nor does it promote in any way a compact of economic solidarity amongst the allies themselves; no arrangement was reached at Paris to adjust the system of the Old World and the New". European governments were pre-occupied with reparations.'

(b) 'The difficulties of regenerating the British economy after the war were enhanced by parts of the Versailles settlement. That "No provision for the economic rehabilitation of Europe," appeared was a profound weakness J. M. Keynes pointed out in *The Economic Consequences of the Peace* (1919). It lacked vision, he further noted, failing to promote ". . . a compact of economic solidarity amongst the allies themselves". Versailles displayed an economic shortsightedness; writing in 1921 R. H. Brand recognised that in the next 5 years reparations would not "be large enough very seriously to alleviate the great financial problems which . . . the nations of Western Europe must have solved".'

In the second example the writer blends the quotations in smoothly; the relevance of the quotation is more explicitly stated. They have both used the same quotation but the first writer takes it wholesale.

When referring to a secondary source, the same care needs to be employed. There are less clumsy ways of using quotations than simply 'the crucial factor in the story of the repeal . . . is the gradual change in Peel's own attitude to the Corn Laws.' (Wood)

'Certainly the Anti-Corn Law League contributed to a stream of tendency for repeal but as A. Wood concludes, "the crucial factor . . . is the gradual change in Peel's own attitude to the Corn Law''. The Anti-Corn Law League may have helped to secure Whig support but what Peel himself called in a letter to Cobden his "sense of public duty" was more influential.'

This is far less crude than the first example and propels the argument forward by its incorporation.

This last example demonstrates elegant interweaving of a shrewd observation. Even if a historian has expressed an idea or answered a question exceptionally well, it is still better in the main to put the same point into your own words. This will give your teacher a better view of your own understanding of those ideas.

> 'The intelligent use of quotations . . . requires skill: too often quotations are thrust into answers in such a way that they distort argument or lead candidates into ever-increasing irrelevance . . . It may be worth mentioning that some candidates achieve Grade 'A' without mentioning any historian or writing down a single quotation.'
> (London University Examiners' Report: A level History, 1981, p.361)

Metaphors

The use of metaphors may enrich understanding, make explicit significance and add colour or style to your writing. As your confidence and understanding increase you will use them in your writing. However you should exercise caution in how far you extend a metaphor. There is a danger that they may become mixed. Debates from the House of Commons provide many instances, as this lesser-known example illustrates:

'The government has thrown down an apple of discord which has burst into flames and flooded the country'. (during the 1902 Education Bill Debate)

Metaphors, when mixed or over extended, may:
1. tend to anachronism.
2. obscure rather than illuminate.
3. misrepresent the truth or your understanding.

What is your opinion of the following examples?

'The Empire had not been a failure, but a great success: and decolonisation proved it. They had recourse again, for the last time, to their favourite 'father and child' analogy. Before, it had justified their arbitrary rule. Now it explained its relaxation. Britain's adopted children had come of age. Her duties as parents had been completed, she had prepared them for the future, they could now stand on their own feet, so she let them go. Of course, there were regrets: no parent ever relinquished power over his children without them. But the object of parenthood was just this, to fit your children for an independent existence. This Britain had done and she should not be dismayed at their majority, but be proud of it, and of the imperialism which had made it possible'.

B. Porter, *The Lion's Share: a short history of British Imperialism 1850–1983* (2nd edition London, 1984) p.339

'Study the historian before you begin to study the facts . . . It is what is already done by the intelligent undergraduate who, when recommended to read a work by that great scholar Jones of St. Jude's, goes round to a friend at St. Jude's to ask what sort of chap Jones is, and what bees he has in his bonnet. When you read a work of history, always listen out for the buzzing. If you can detect none, either you are tone deaf or your historian is a dull dog. The facts are really not at all like a fish on the fishmonger's slab. They are like fish swimming about in a vast and sometimes inaccessible ocean, and what the historian catches will depend, partly on chance, but mainly on what part of the ocean he chooses to fish in and what tackle he chooses to use—these two factors being, of course, determined by the kind of fish he wants to catch. By and large, the historian will get the kind of facts he wants. History means interpretation.

E. H. Carr, *What is History* (Harmondsworth, 1964) p.23

Lastly a simple point of style, which affects the impression gained of an essay. You are encouraged to express your own ideas in essays and many questions demand it. But the bold announcement 'I think that . . .' seems to imply that you are undergoing a temporary mental disorder and very shortly you will revert to normal. All of your essays should be the product of thought. Even when referring to personal opinion it is not normally considered good style to do so directly. The essay should seek to be an objective discussion; references to 'I' do not lead to that impression. As long as a strong argument or sound reasons are given for your opinions they will stand on their own. Consider the following two sentences:

—'I think that the influence of the Anti-Corn Law League has been exaggerated.'
—'The influence of the Anti-Corn Law League has been exaggerated'.

The first example has not gained anything from introducing 'I think that . . .'; the second has not lost anything by omitting it.

The Conclusion

You will remember that we referred to the essay as a journey. By the time you write the conclusion-you will have reached your destination. The purpose of the conclusion is to remind the reader of what you have accomplished during the essay. The conclusion is not supposed to be a bland endorsement of the essay title or a simple restatement of what has gone before.

It is important to:

1. state clearly your main idea, argument or explanation, i.e. what seems most important to you in your answer.

2. show *how* and *why* the argument or answer you have offered differs from, or qualifies, the essay title.

By all means refer to the wording of the title to make clear the importance of your answer to the question sct. Say how and why your answer relates to:

1. the title.

2. your intentions as set out in the introduction.

Try to avoid being overcome by the sense of relief at finishing which produces a vague summary or a conclusion of the 'thus it can be seen . . .' variety.

The conclusion to your essay will be determined by what has preceded it. Some of the best conclusions are short and very much to the point. Use a maximum of 8–10 lines or 6–7 sentences. Again this is helpful because it contains and defines the conclusion.

> The conclusion must confront the title with your main point or argument to show that you have satisfied the question.

This last example of a conclusion is lengthy but notice how it confronts the question.

Account for the outbreak of the Civil War in Spain.

'The outbreak of the Spanish Civil War must be understood in the context of traditional society and the economic stresses it suffered in the 1920's and 1930's. The Republic had supplanted a symbolic structural feature—the monarchy, it attacked another—the church and expected the compliance of the army. The Republic's dealing with the fundamental institutions undermined its consensus, "everything and at once" was "too much, too quickly". The Republic was not strong, it did not have a middle class to support and stabilise it. Crucially the second Republic failed to materially improve the lot of the majority of the Spanish people who lost faith in it and eventually rejected it. War was a recourse for Spaniards hoping eventually for radical solutions to Spain's long term economic and political problems.'

There are various ways of finishing the essay. You can use a sensible hypothesis or question, perhaps even a little outside the specifications of your present title. A poignant or shrewd quotation may consolidate or embellish your final remarks.

Consider the following final sentences:

(a) It is tempting to see the Boer War not as ending British Imperialism but as turning its energy inwards. Imperialism, therefore, had to be built on the 'efficiency of the nation'. The white man's burden had to be carried on strong backs.

(b) There can be no doubt that as a result of the Boer War the 20th century in England, opened in a sense of national doubt. Arguably, one casualty, the Liberal Party, was to be fatally wounded in the next and Greater conflict.

(c) The Boer War proved most dramatically Chamberlain's prophetic words in 1898 when he noted, "we are the most powerful Empire in the world, but we are not *all powerful*".

(d) 'The saddest result of the Boer War was that the Liberal government approved a most illiberal constitution for the South Africa Union in settlements of 1906 and 1910. Racial politics were as distasteful then as now but were as the government put it "part of an essential compromise". Herbert Samuel argued in 1902 "the only guarantee of an empire's unity is the contentedness of the people who compose it". The Liberals' magnanimity cost dear.'

Remember the conclusion is the final part of your essay. It is bound to leave an impression.

'The conclusion . . . marks the end, the rounding off, of an argument and its value lies both in reminding the reader succinctly of what has been written and in endeavouring to create, with the reader, a favourable impression and a disposition to treat favourably.'
(J.M.B. Examiners' Report:
A level History, 1980, p.19)

The Essay Writing Process

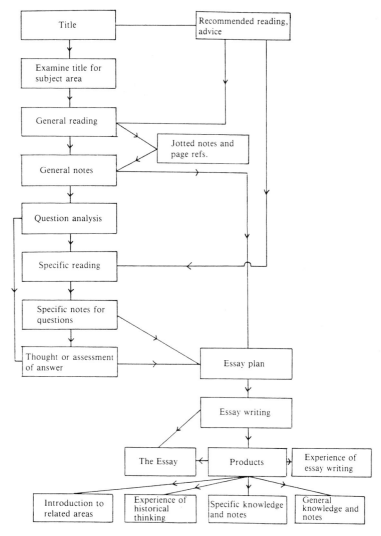

(This flow chart shows the student's unaided progress in producing an essay from being given a title and reading list.

D. CHECKLIST

1. Prepare your notes carefully and thoroughly.

2. Remember the use of historical knowledge to answer the question set is vital —Relevance!

3. Plan your essay.

4. Learn from each essay, not only about the period, but also how you are developing the skill of essay writing.

5. Introductions are important for writer and reader. Make sure a relevant line of argument appears in the introduction.

6. Structure your essay into a predetermined number of paragraphs.

7. Do not be afraid to leave something out if it does not fit!

8. Make sure the reader knows why you are including pieces of information. Make it explicit.

9. Remember the model of 'statement— reasons'.

10. Ask questions of everything you write to make sure it is relevant, accurate and clear.

11. Read widely for historical knowledge and to improve your English.

12. Check spellings just as you would check your facts.

13. The conclusion should remind the reader of what you have accomplished. Confront the title with your main point to show how you have satisfied the question.

EVIDENCE

About this Chapter

This chapter will deal with the types of written historical evidence and its problems. It will then establish a hierarchy of skills in the use of documents, and will indicate the types of question which exercise those skills. Most important of all, the chapter contains exercises so that the practice of using historical evidence can reinforce this vital aspect of historical study.

'The historian must carry out an exhaustive search of available evidence.'

A. THE IMPORTANCE OF EVIDENCE

The Task of the Historian

Evidence is the raw material of History, and can be the starting point in the process of historical inquiry. The historian uses many different sources of information, written and non-written, to construct his interpretation of the past. These sources are here referred to as 'evidence', meaning the sources themselves and the use to which the historian puts them in order to support or prove his interpretations. This historical process involves three principal stages:

1. Examine as much of the available evidence as is possible.

2. Ask questions of that evidence.
       For example—where does it originate?
                   —is it reliable?
                   —is it complete?
                   —is it useful?

3. Draw conclusions to construct an objective view of the past.

The idea of an 'objective view' may suggest that there is one true body of knowledge which makes up History. Of course, this is a false assumption.

One of the fascinations of History is the variety of evidence and interpretation available to writers and readers.

Views of what happened in the past will vary.

1. The evidence does not speak for itself. It is the historian who decides which evidence he will select and reject, and the choice will depend on:

   (a) the skill of the historian.
   (b) the historian's views about what kind of evidence is important.
   (c) the evidence that is known about and available to the historian at the time of writing.
   (d) the purpose of the historian.

2. The conclusions which historians draw are in themselves controversial.

   (a) They depend on the evidence and how it is used.
   (b) They are essentially personal, and although historians may try to be objective and impartial they cannot free themselves entirely from their own ideas about people and the world, their personal likes and dislikes, and the assumptions and values of the age in which they live.

The study of Advanced level History is concerned with all of these processes. For you, all historical writing must be thought of as evidence. Some of this evidence will derive from the time of the event, some of it will appear in a standard text book, or a more specialised monograph (see Analytical Reading, p.10).

You will have to consider the evidence, select from it, and add your own interpretation according to the demands of a specific task—a set essay for example. Until recently, at A level 'the evidence' has mainly consisted of historians' work; a text book could be taken as the whole truth. Increasingly, evidence-based questions are being used which add two new dimensions to your study of history:

1. It is far more important to examine original source material, and not just the work of historians.

2. It is important to understand the problematic nature of historical evidence, its advantages and failings, its certainties and its contentions.

Primary and Secondary Evidence

Primary evidence is first-hand information about an event, not based on other sources. Secondary evidence is second-hand information, removed in time and/or place from the incident referred to. Both types have their advantages and their drawbacks in the way that they contribute to accurate historical explanation.

Primary evidence is the point of origin of all historical thought and writing. However, it needs to be understood in its context, and requires critical examination before it can be used to write History. For example, consider the circumstances of the writer. A mineworker may have a valuable view of the effect of the General Strike on his pit, and in his town, but may know little of the broader picture. Lenin, with his wealth of information about the situation in Russia in 1917, would tend to interpret that information from one perspective. A news sequence made at the time of the invasion of Suez in 1956 may present gripping pictures, but is likely to say what the audience of the day wants to hear. Thus we cannot rely solely on a single source, that is, the evidence given by one person. The historian's job is to judge the reliability and value of each source in turn, and by consulting all available sources, to build up a complete picture.

Secondary evidence can broadly be subdivided:

1. Contemporary, or near contemporary second-hand evidence. While not present at an event, the writer may have been able to use his own detailed sources which are no longer available —or the writer may have relied on hearsay. This sort of evidence should be carefully examined for what it is worth.

2. The work of historians writing in recent times, using evidence available today. If the historian has been attempting to seek the truth, such work should have breadth and balance.

However, not all historians set out with this purpose. A British historian writing in 1900 may have written under the influence of a glorious Empire, or ardent early socialism. An historian writing today, in a country where truth is influenced by ideology, will not write objectively. At the most extreme, consider how History was written in Orwell's '1984'. The historian, just as much as contemporaries, may write with a purpose in mind, with a particular point to make, and is just as subject to the influences, ideas and circumstances of the age in which he lives. History, then, may serve many masters other than the principle of an objective, 'total' reconstruction of past reality.

Documentary questions in the Advanced level examination will usually present both primary and secondary evidence. The best way to prepare for this is to work through the same processes as historians working with a wide range of documents.

B. THE HISTORIAN'S PROCEDURE

The historian must:

1. come to terms with the language and style of the document.

2. understand its meaning and its implications, both in terms of content and context.

3. assess its reliability and value.

4. select relevant information.

5. make inferences and draw conclusions, either from the document on its own or alongside other documents.

Making Sense of Documents

REWORDING

Students studying twentieth century history may find problems with certain types of documents, but only because of specialised language or the verbosity of the writer. However, nineteenth century documents are far more demanding, often having complex and unfamiliar sentence structure, and changes in the meaning of certain words. When you are working with documents which display these difficulties, make a point of clarifying them by rewriting the passage in your own words. If a meaning cannot be obtained from the context, consult a dictionary which provides archaic meanings.

THE TRIPLE ALLIANCE

A1.	The triple alliance which I originally sought to conclude after the peace of Frankfurt and about which I had already sounded Vienna and St. Petersburg in September 1870, was an alliance of the three Emperors with the further idea of bringing into it monarchical Italy. It was designed for the struggle which, as I feared, was before us; between the two European tendencies which Napoleon I called Republican and Cossack, and which I, according to our present ideas, should designate on the one side as the system of order on a monarchical basis, and on the other as the social republic to the level of which the anti-monarchical development is wont to sink, either slowly or by leaps and bounds, until the conditions thus created become intolerable, and the disappointed populace are ready for a violent return to monarchical institutions in a Caesarean form.

Bismarck, *Reflections and Reminiscences* (1898)

A2. The Triple Alliance, which I first tried to arrange after the Franco-Prussian War, and about which I had already approached Austria and Russia in 1870, was an alliance of three Emperors, with the further idea of including the King of Italy. Its purpose was to prepare for the coming struggle between good order under a monarchy, and the revolutionary socialism of the sort to which republics often sink—until, that is, conditions deteriorate to the point where people are ready to revolt against the system and return to the rule of an even more powerful dictator.

PRÉCIS: WRITING A SUMMARY

Another strategy for improving skills with documents is to précis a passage. Many documents, especially from the nineteenth century, contain redundant words which only serve to confuse. By writing a précis you boil a passage down to its essentials, and the meaning should then be crystal clear!

Study these examples of rewording and précis.

LENIN IN SWITZERLAND

B1	Lenin, addressing Swiss workers shortly before his departure for Russia in 1917.
	We said that if the revolution is victorious in Russia and a republican government comes to power which wants to continue the imperialist war in alliance with the imperialist bourgeoisie of England and France, a war for the conquest of Constantinople, Armenia, Galicia, and so on and so forth, then we will be decided opponents of such a government, we will be against "the defence of the Fatherland" in such a war.
	Now such an eventuality has arisen. The new government of Russia which negotiated with the brother of Nicholas II with a view to restoring the monarchy in Russia, and in which the leading monarchists Lvov and Guchkov occupy leading positions, this government is trying to represent as a defensive war . . . its imperialist war with Germany, to represent as a defence of the Russian republic . . . the defence of the predatory imperialist bandit-like aims of Russian, English, and other capital.
	Lenin Sochineniya, Vol XX, p.66.

B2 We said that if the new revolutionary government wanted to continue to fight an imperialist war alongside England and France with conquest in mind, we would oppose them.

This has now happened. The new government, with strong Tsarist influence, is pretending to fight a war to defend the republic when all it is really defending is its aim of conquest and profit.

A2 is a straightforward rewording, conveying the meaning of the original sentence by sentence. B2 is a précis, giving only a summary of the original. Rewording is a worthwhile exercise because it forces you to come to terms with language. Précis is even better because the process enhances understanding.

The essential purposes of a précis are:

1. to identify the important message.

2. to reduce the number of words.

A POSSIBLE METHOD OF WORKING

1. To identify the important message:

(a) Establish the subject matter of the document.
(b) Identify the subordinate material, such as evidence used in support.
(c) Assess the relative importance of the different parts of the document.
(d) Recognise the medium of the message—for example, the style, language, form or mode of expression may in themselves be of importance, and some attempt should be made to convey them in the précis.
(e) Acknowledge and convey the nature and purpose of the document.

2. To reduce the number of words:

(a) Select the words which seem to you to be important for retaining the important messages of the document—key words, points of understanding or argument, main points in support.
(b) Reject those words which obscure rather than clarify meaning—words which are only present for purposes of style, linguistic sense, grammar, or form.
(c) Change words and phrases into modern meanings. The substitutes must be able to express the purpose and significance of the originals, and must therefore be carefully chosen.

(d) Summarise the words which remain, putting the sense of the document in your own way.
(e) Reorganise into a logical order—there is no guarantee that the original (being an extract) will be logical. Bring the main points to the fore, keeping subordinate material in its place. This creates a structure which clarifies the message of the document.

Placing a Document in Context

One of the important skills in the use of historical evidence is to place a document, and specific references within it, into the broader context of surrounding events and ideas. Context questions will require that the student be able to:

1. recognise the events and ideas referred to in the document.

2. understand the implications of what the document is saying, for example, to give the meaning of a particular phrase, sentence, or idea in other words.

3. use background knowledge to set the document in its place and make sense of it.

To cope with such a question you must:

(a) have read widely and possess a thorough knowledge of the course.

(b) have the patience to search for helpful clues.

(c) pay attention to mark distribution and allocate examination time (and proportion of information given) accordingly.

EXERCISE

The following extract, and the questions after it, are typical of context questions in terms of depth of detail and range of knowledge required.

THE CONSTITUTIONAL CRISIS OF 1909

In all seriousness, my Lords, we have a right to ask where this kind of thing is going to stop. If you can graft Licensing Bills and Land Valuation Bills and measures of that kind on *the Finance Bill*, what is to prevent you grafting on it, let us say, a *Home Rule Bill*—setting up an authority in Ireland to collect and dispense all the taxes of that country? There is literally no limit to the abuses which might creep in if such a practice were allowed to go on without restriction. Upon this ground alone I venture to think that your Lordship's House might consider very seriously whether you are justified in passing this Bill into Law . . .

I trust . . . I have said enough to show your lordships that the question before you is not whether you can reject this Bill but whether you ought to reject this Bill—a wholly different thing. You have to consider its results as they would affect all classes of the community, and the principles that underlie it, and you have to consider *whether the people of this country* have *been consulted with regard to it.* If you find that the results are likely to be disastrous, and that the principles underlying it, which we detect not only from the official utterances of members of the Government but also from the more indiscreet explanations of so-called supporters of the government are pernicious and that the whole matter is one that has never been duly referred to the people of this country, then I venture to say that your Lordships have a clear duty before you—not to decree the final extinction of the Bill—because that is not what we propose, but to insist that before it becomes law an authoritative expression of the opinion of the electors of the United Kingdom shall have reached us with regard to it.

We shall be asked whether we have considered the consequences of rejecting the Budget. My Lords, we have considered them and we are ready to face them.

Lord Lansdowne, speech to the House of Lords, November 1909.

1. What position was held by Lord Lansdowne at this time?

2. What were the circumstances which preceded the introduction of the Finance Bill in 1909?

3. How does Lord Lansdowne justify the rejection of the Bill with regard to
   a) the content of the Bill itself?
   b) the constitution?

4. What indications are there that Lansdowne wishes to pursue a cautious policy, and how would you explain that caution?

5. What were the consequences of the rejection of the Bill?

With the exception of (3) all these questions rely on background knowledge, and the evidence itself acts as a stimulus. Therefore the answers are closed and can be found by reference to a suitable book. If you do not know the answers already, use this as a research exercise.

The Reliability of Documents

Whereas the context or stimulus question is largely concerned with location and knowledge, some examination boards set questions which are concerned solely with the evidence itself; in this type of question, the use of background knowledge is prohibited. What the questions seek is a demonstration of the student's understanding of the nature and complexity of historical evidence.

EXTERNAL CLUES

When confronted with any evidence, the historian has to establish its reliability—whether it is accurate, full, and consistent with available knowledge. Certain key questions can be asked of evidence as guides to reliability.

The source or place of origin of a document should be given at the head or foot. Sometimes it may contain information about the author, the date, the writer's access to information, and even the purpose of the writer, which are clues for the historian about the source's reliability.

EXAMPLES

Primary Sources:

Ireland For Ever, by General F. P. Crozier, 1932.

The title is in itself very revealing, and a Unionist commander is unlikely to achieve objectivity, however much the book may bring a vivid account of the events with which Crozier was concerned.

C. F. G. Masterman, by L. Masterman, 1937.

Can a politician's wife (or husband) achieve objectivity?

Secondary Sources:

Great Contemporaries, by W. S. Churchill, 1932.

Such a title, and a book written by a political figure at a time of great controversy . . .

The General Strike, by W. H. Crook, 1931.

The title is fine, and the author's name should not be held against him. The problem here is the date. A book written so close to the time is unlikely to have achieved the necessary perspective on such a controversial subject and not all of the evidence will have been accessible. Furthermore, the interpretations of historians will have long since superceded the ideas of W. H. Crook. The more recent, the better!

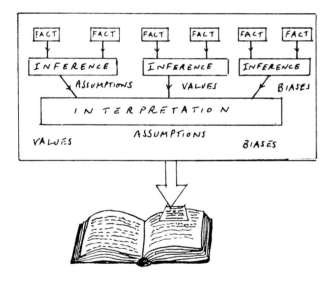

INTERNAL CLUES

What is the Factual Content of the Document?

For our purposes, facts may be defined as statements which are accepted to be true and may be supported by evidence. The specific statement 'The General Strike took place in May 1926' is clearly factual. In a broader sense, so too is the statement, 'The General Strike, one of the greatest clashes between government and Unions in British history, took place in May 1926.' On the other hand to say that 'The General Strike was an attempt by the Trade Unions to blackmail the government' is not a fact. It cannot be supported by evidence. A fact, by this definition, must be true. Generally speaking, a document which presents factual material in volume and with precision encourages the reader to believe in its reliability.

Even so, caution is required:

1. Some sources, especially primary ones, may contain statements made in error. A witness writing about an event which happened long before, or a witness using hearsay, rather than first hand experience of an event, might unintentionally make errors.

2. Facts which are individually correct may be used together to distort a picture. This can be the outcome of (a) a process which selects only those facts which prove a given case, and omits others—an intentional distortion of evidence; or (b) an unwitting omission, a failure to carry out the exhaustive search for evidence which should characterise historical study.

For these reasons, even the facts contained in documents need to be checked.

How Balanced are the Interpretations?

History is not, of course, made up entirely of facts. The job of the historian is to go beyond the facts, and to make interpretations. These interpretations will fill gaps, clarify, explain, and provide an overall view.

1. The scope of interpretation.

At one extreme, the process of interpretation will simply involve the making of inferences from two or more documents.

EXAMPLE

One source may say:

'The Bolshevik programme demanded peace, bread and land.'

A second source may say:

'Russian peasants and workers wanted peace, bread and land'.

The simple inference from these documents is that peasants and workers supported the bolsheviks. Subsequent evidence may confirm or deny that inference.

At the other extreme, the scope of interpretation can be vast. A historical idea such as 'Victorianism' or 'The Scramble for Africa' is a major piece of historical interpretation. Broadly speaking, interpretations can be classified into two groups: judgements and opinions. Often the distinction between the two will be blurred, but they may be tested by the following criteria:

JUDGEMENTS	OPINIONS
Should be objective.	May be subjective.
Should be even-handed, acknowledging alternative views	May be argued from one viewpoint
Should be made on the basis of what is known.	May speculate on the unknown on the basis of what is known.
Can largely be supported by evidence.	May be made without evidence in support.
May acknowledge opinions.	Are unlikely to acknowledge judgements.
Should be the result of rational thought processes.	May be affected by one's beliefs or feelings.
On these grounds, judgements are more likely to impress than opinions.	

Do not assume, however, that all judgements are automatically good and opinions bad. Judgements may be poor, opinions may be sound and all interpretations should be assessed on their merits.

2. The reliability of interpretations.

When you are considering the reliability of interpretations, bear these points in mind:

— How far can the statement be supported by known evidence?

— Can you appreciate the reasoning behind an interpretation?

— How balanced, fair, truthful or objective does a statement seem to be? Clues which will help you to establish this may include the suspended judgement ('it may be that . . .', 'perhaps . . .', 'the evidence suggests . . .') — encouraging; or the presence of sarcasm, exaggeration, a dominating tone—discouraging.

EXAMPLE

In assessing interpretations, you should be cautious. Sometimes the historian will make statements, but legitimately through lack of space of relevance may *omit details of evidence and his reasoning*. In the first example, Evans makes

legitimate but undoubtedly sweeping interpretations which are only substantiated later in his book.

'The historian's job is to judge the reliability and value of each source in turn.'

BENJAMIN DISRAELI

'He had decided to make politics his real career, though the handicaps were enormous. He was a nobody. He was poor. He had been neither to a great school nor to a university. He was a Jew. For such a man to assault the Government citadel, garrisoned by aristocrats, and buttressed by wealth, seemed mere madness. On the other hand, he had great gifts. Superb courage and unlimited patience supported an altogether exceptional political intelligence, and in both speech and writing he could express his beliefs with all the brilliance of a highly original mind . . .

Within twelve years of his entry into Parliament Disraeli had become the leader of the Tory Party in the House of Commons: an amazing achievement, due partly to an unforeseen political cataclysm, but in the main to sheer political skill, patience and courage.'

R. Evans, *The Victorian Age*, (London, 1950) p.193

Evans would support these interpretations in depth in the course of his book, and they may well prove valid.

Alternatively an historian may select that evidence which matches the interpretation which he or she wants to put on it. This is a distortion of historical truth, and the student of history must look out for clues which reveal its unreliability.

Read this account of the Fascist rally at Olympia, 1934, and consider the questions in the exercise which follows.

EXERCISE: FASCISM 1934

A.   'Old gang support of mob rule against fascism reached its height over the huge Olympia meeting held by Mosley in 1934. Perhaps the mightiest indoor rally ever held in Britain, Mosley had no sooner begun to speak than it became clear that organised Red gangs, each hundreds strong, were occupying positions in every part of the huge arena . . . with the sole intention of preventing the speech being heard. Five or six in one part of the hall would create a din, and when Blackshirt stewards approached to eject them scores of Red colleagues would arise to join in the battle. There would be a fierce struggle, resulting in the Reds being bundled out of the building, whereupon the same tactics would be employed in another part of the building. So it went on for two long hours during which the thousands present learned nothing about Fascism except the bravery and pertinacity of its young adherents in dealing with this very perilous situation.'

A. K. Chesterton, *Oswald Mosley, Portrait of a Leader*

1. Does the citation give any external clues about the reliability of the document?

2. Where does the writer make clear his view of

   i) Mosley?

   ii) his opponents?

3. Which particular words and phrases show that the writer is stating opinions rather than making judgements?

IS THERE ANY CONTRADICTION BETWEEN DOCUMENTS?

The document should have provoked a number of doubts in your mind. To further test the reliability of the account, and to find the truth about what happened, the student must move away from one document to a comparison between different sources of evidence. Where two sources agree, confidence in them will be further encouraged. Where they are contradictory a decision of some sort must be made, or further evidence found to determine the issue.

Compare this account of the Olympia rally with Chesterton's account in Source A

B. 'At 8.45 Mosley began to speak. "Ladies and gentlemen . . . this meeting, the largest indoor meeting ever held under one roof in Britain, is the culmination of a great national campaign in which audiences of every city in this land have gathered to hear the fascist case . . .''

At this point the first disturbance broke out in one of the galleries, with groups of men and women starting to chant "Fascism means murder: Down with Mosley". The speaker paused in his speech and warned that if they did not stop they would be removed. The shouting continued, and Mosley then ordered the stewards into action. The interrupters were removed, but as soon as he had started to speak again further shouting took place from another quarter of the building. Again the offenders were removed . . .

The same evening Mosley and Gerald Barry, editor of the News Chronicle, and a former enthusiast for the new party's economic programme, made statements on Olympia on the B.B.C. . . . Mosley produced what was to become the standard fascist defence. The communists had organised to break up Olympia. They rose in "Highly organised groups" to "shout down free speech". They attacked his men with every kind of "vile weapon". "Now I put it to you, to your sense of fair play: would you have handled these Reds very gently? When you have seen your men kicked in the stomach and slashed with razors, and your women with their faces streaming with blood?" Gerald Barry had seen no such weapons but had observed single interrupters "being struck on the head, in the stomach, and all over the body with a complete absence of restraint". Nor were these actions confined to the auditorium. The worst atrocities took place in the corridors running off the hall where he had been horrified to see "a man lying on the floor, obviously powerless and done for, being mercilessly kicked and horribly handled by a group of Blackshirts". The violence of this and a similar incident was greater than "anything I have seen in my life short of war".

R. Skidelsky, *Oswald Mosley*, (London, 1975)

1. Does source B give any more grounds for confidence in the document than source A?

2. Are there any points of agreement between the two documents?

3. What are the principal differences of interpretation?

4. What aspects of the internal evidence encourage greater confidence in the reliability of this document? Look in particular at

    (a) the style and methodology of the writer

    (b) the sources of information used

    (c) the amount of fine detail

Rarely will evidence such as source A condemn itself so readily, and rarely will interpretation differ to this extreme. Clearly one source is unreliable, and the interpretations which it offers are heavily biased. One may conclude that the motive of the writer was to add to the growing fascist propaganda which appeared in the 1920s and 1930s. Therefore source A does not reflect the historian's concern to make informed judgements about the past.

Synthesis, Inference, and Interpretations

Having consulted all available evidence and carefully examined it for reliability, the historian has to decide, judge, evaluate and interpret in a final summary or synthesis. By the same process you too will have to produce a synthesis from a more limited range of documents. Synthesis is the process of blending a number of pieces of evidence together into one coherent account. It requires an element of direct involvement because of the need for selection and weighing of evidence, but the whole product should be no more than the sum of the parts. You will not have added anything of your own.

However, even historians who do search for truth may disagree in their interpretation of an event. This will especially be true where the problem is a complex one, such as an investigation in historical causation. Where eminent historians argue, the student can do little more than be aware of the conflict of ideas.

A famous example concerns the origins of the Second World War. Read these two interpretations, and consider the exercises which follow.

A

'The settlement at Munich was a triumph for British policy, which had worked precisely to this end; not a triumph for Hitler, who had started with no such clear intention. Nor was it merely a triumph for selfish or cynical British statesmen, indifferent to the fate of far-off peoples or calculating that Hitler might be launched into war against Soviet Russia. It was a triumph for all that was best and most enlightened in British life; a triumph for those who had preached equal justice between peoples; a triumph for those who had courageously denounced the harshness and short-sightedness of Versailles. Brailsford, the leading socialist authority on foreign affairs, wrote in 1920 of the peace settlement: "The worst offence was the subjection of over three million Germans to Czech rule." This was the offence redressed at Munich. Idealists could claim that British policy had been tardy and hesitant. In 1938 it atoned for these failings. With skill and persistence, Chamberlain brought first the French, and then the Czechs, to follow the moral line.'

A. J. P. Taylor, *The Origins of the Second World War*, (Harmondsworth, 1964) p.234

B

'Hitler's prestige rose to new heights in Germany, where relief that war had been avoided was combined with delight in the gains that had been won on the cheap . . .

Abroad the effect was equally startling, and Mr. Churchill described the results of the Munich settlement in a famous speech on 5 October 1938:

At Berchtesgaden . . . £1 was demanded at the pistol's point. When it was given (at Godesberg), £2 was demanded at the pistol's point. Finally the Dictator consented to take £1 17s 6d. and the rest in promises for the future . . . We are in the presence of a disaster of the first magnitude.

Austria and the Sudetenland within six months represented the triumph of those methods of political warfare which Hitler had so sedulously applied in the past five years. His diagnosis of the weakness of the Western democracies, and of the international divisions which prevented the formation of a united front against him, had been brilliantly vindicated . . .

The fact that the Prime Minister of Great Britain had twice flown to Germany to intercede with him, and on the third occasion had hurried across Europe with the heads of the French and Italian Governments to meet him at the shortest possible notice, constituted a personal triumph for Hitler.

A. Bullock, *Hitler, A Study in Tyranny*, (Harmondsworth, 1952)

EXERCISES

1. Compare and explain the two interpretations of the Munich settlement with particular reference to

   (a) the aims and methods of Hitler,
   (b) the aims and methods of Chamberlain,
   (c) which of them was successful.

2. Is there any way of finding which of them is right?

These cases show the need for caution when dealing with interpretations. Remember that they are not absolute. When you begin to interpret documents, do not commit yourself to definite statements. Acknowledge in your wording— 'possibly', 'maybe', 'one explanation ...'—that there is room for other points of view or that evidence is insufficient to admit of confident verdicts.

THE USEFULNESS OF DOCUMENTS

The emphasis of the last section was on reliability. Reliability should not be confused with usefulness. When looking at reliability one principal concern was the purpose of the writer— whether of a primary or secondary source. When considering value the principal concern is the use to which that evidence will be put.

Case Study: The End of the Labour Government, 1931

Source A

On Friday 21st there was a long cabinet meeting. Agreement on economies to be proposed by Parliament was reached, the crisis was apparently over, and the members dispersed to their weekend retreats. The economies, however, still amounted to only £56 millions ... The Liberals ... and Conservatives returned to MacDonald late that evening and told him that the economies were quite inadequate, and unlikely to be accepted by Parliament or to restore confidence. Chamberlain told MacDonald that, in such circumstances, the financial crash would come before Parliament met, and it was therefore his duty to avoid it; for which purpose the Conservatives (and Samuel endorsed this for the Liberals) would give him all their support in the present government or in a 'reconstructed' government. MacDonald spoke of his difficulties with characteristic self-pity, but said he would not resign, but go on with those of his colleagues who would follow him[1].

Hence another Cabinet meeting on Saturday, the 22nd ... to try to agree on additional economies which would win Opposition support. These, so MacDonald and Snowden told their colleagues, must amount to £25–30 millions, the bulk of them to be found out of unemployment charges ... only reductions in unemployment payments would satisfy the opposition and resolve the crisis; yet this would at the same time betray the hopes of the party's supporters and probably split the party itself ... The meeting did however, authorise ... hypothetical economies of 68.5 millions, including 12.5 millions saved by a 10% reduction in unemployment allowances.

MacDonald saw the King at ten o'clock. He explained the need for further credits from New York ... He warned, however, that some of the ministers, and especially Henderson and Graham, would not accept such economies, and that their resignations would necessitate the resignation of the entire government. On hearing this, the King decided to consult the leaders of the opposition parties, Baldwin and Samuel[2].

At noon the King saw Sir Herbert Samuel at the Palace. Samuel strongly advised that MacDonald should be persuaded to stay on as head of the existing government or some 'reconstituted' Labour Cabinet or, failing these alternatives, of a National government made up of members of the three parties; the necessary but unpalatable economies affecting the working class could best be imposed by a Labour government. Baldwin ... declared his readiness to serve the country, either in a National government or in a Conservative government with Liberal support[3].

The critical meeting of the Cabinet was held at seven that evening (Sunday, August 23) ...At 8.45 a telephone message came from the Bank of England, followed by the telegram from New York. MacDonald read it to the members of the Cabinet (imposing further conditions before a loan would be given).

MacDonald appealed to his colleagues to accept the larger economies ... The alternative, if any senior ministers wished to resign, was the resignation of the whole Cabinet. The figure involved was a paltry £12.25 millions. Yet it involved a principle which many could not accept: regardless of the sacrifices demanded of the rest of the community, it seemed too much to ask of the poorest of the poor. There was complete deadlock. Eleven ministers were ready to support the reduction in unemployment payments; ten were not.

During these discussions MacDonald had nothing to contribute. He sat back, absent-mindedly doodling on a blotter, waiting wearily for the end.[4] ''When this final disagreement occurred'' wrote Snowden, it was evident that the Prime Minister had anticipated such a development and had made his plans to deal with it''. He asked the members of the Cabinet to place their resignations in his hands, which they did. He then left to see the King ... The Cabinet then dispersed, expecting that next day another government, presumably a Conservative-Liberal coalition, would be formed ...

On Monday, August 24, after a meeting with the King in the morning, MacDonald met his Cabinet once more, at noon. He told it, to its utter stupefaction, that though it was out, he was in; that he had agreed to head a National government composed of individuals rather than parties, as a temporary expedient for the sole purpose of settling the financial crisis; Baldwin and Samuel were prepared to join.'

1. K. Feiling, *N. Chamberlain*, pp.191–3; P. Snowden, *Autobiography*, II, 938–40, Samuel in Parliament, Sept. 14, 1931.
2. H. Nicolson, *George V*, pp.460–1.
3. Ibid., pp.461–2; Lord Samuel, *Grooves of Change*, p.246.
4. L. M. Weir, *Tragedy of Ramsey MacDonald*, p.382.

from Charles Loch Mowat, *Britain between the Wars*, (London, 1955)

Source B

'When the Labour government as a whole declined to agree to a reduction of unemployment pay, Mr. MacDonald assumed too hurriedly that this involved the resignation of his government. He neither showed nor expressed any grief at this regrettable development. On the contrary, he set about the formation of the National government with an enthusiasm which showed that the adventure was highly agreeable to him.

Taking all these things together, I think they give ground for the suspicion expressed by Mr. Henderson and other Labour ministers that Mr. MacDonald had deliberately planned the scheme of a National government; which would at the same time enable him to retain the position of Prime Minister and to associate with colleagues with whom he was more in sympathy than he had ever been with his Labour colleagues ... His mind for a long time before this crisis arose had been turning to the idea of a new party orientation and government by what he called a Council of State ... I remember a statement (Mr. Baldwin) had made two or three years before, that probably the time was not too far distant when he and Mr MacDonald would be sitting in the same Cabinet.'

from Philip Viscount Snowden, *An Autobiography*, (London, 1934)

Source C

'The impression left on the minds of those who heard the speech, after the first sensations of surprise had passed, was that the whole thing had been arranged long before and that, while in the Cabinet and committee they had been making panic-stricken efforts to balance the budget, the whole business had been a humbug and make-believe.'

taken from L. H. Weir, *The Tragedy of Ramsay MacDonald*, (1938)

Source D

'Shortly after the Cabinet dispersed SB went to Downing Street in response to a request from MacDonald. Samuel had already arrived and within a few minutes they were joined by Neville Chamberlain, MacDonald told them of the situation in the Cabinet, and of his advice to the King. It was quite clear that he intended to resign and that he had no intention of joining a coalition, even though the King had urged him to head one. Neville, however, pressed on him the support in the country that he would bring to such an administration, and the effect it would have in restoring confidence. His arguments seemed to have no effect. To everyone else at the meeting it seemed quite certain that MacDonald intended to resign and SB returned from it convinced that he would have to form a government.'

from Sir John Davidson's draft memoirs, quoted in Humphrey Berkeley, *The Myth that will not Die*, (1978). Davidson was a close friend and confidant of Stanley Baldwin.

Source E

I explained (to the King) my hopeless party position if there were any number of resignations. He said he believed I was the only person who could carry the country through. I said that, did I share his belief, I should not contemplate what I do, but that I did not share it.

from MacDonald's diary, also quoted in *The Myth that will not Die*.

Source F

'This defeat in the October 1931 election is still very much a part of the mythology of the Labour movement. For Labour supporters, 1931 was the election when the party went down to a cataclysmic and catastrophic defeat, betrayed by MacDonald and deserted by its working class supporters ... The reason for this mistaken mythology is not difficult to find. For both historians and activists at the time, Labour's defeat in the 1931 and MacDonald's "betrayal" are inseparable ... (Yet) a Labour reverse was almost inevitable ...'

from Stevenson and Cook, *The Slump*, (1977)

QUESTIONS

Read Source A.

1. What were the respective positions of MacDonald, Samuel, Baldwin, and Snowden?

2. What circumstances created the need for the economies referred to in line 6?

3. Why was the issue of economies one of so much difficulty for the Labour Party?

4. Does the writer make any judgements about:
   a) the character of MacDonald,
   b) MacDonald's attitude towards a national government?

5. What aspects of this narrative would add to, or undermine, your confidence in the writer?

   In his book, Mowat proceeds to a detailed analysis of the part played by MacDonald in the crisis. Did he plan to form a national government, or was it an expedient forced upon him by circumstances? To follow the same process of enquiry, consider sources B-F.

6. Refer to source B. What evidence does Snowden give to prove his assertion that MacDonald had planned for a National government?

7. What is the attitude of Snowden towards MacDonald as revealed by this extract?

8. Do you consider the evidence in the extract to be reliable?

9. Does this extract cause you to ask any new questions about the material in source A?

10. Does the tone and content of source C add weight to Snowden's argument?

11. Refer to sources D and E. How do they contradict the arguments expressed in B and C?

12. Consider the origin of both of these sources, and comment on their value in resolving this question.

13. Refer to source F. According to this source, did MacDonald deserve accusations of betrayal? What aspects of the source encourage belief in its reliability?

14. Use the evidence above to answer the question, "Did MacDonald plan the formation of a National Government?"

Finally, what was Mowat's judgement? "His decision, then, at the height of the crisis, is not hard to understand. That he decided upon it earlier, as opposed to being vaguely predisposed to it, cannot be proven."

COMMENTARY

1–3. These are context questions which test knowledge and understanding. If you don't know the answers, go and find out!

4. (a) On MacDonald's character you should have indicated the telling phrase 'characteristic self-pity' and indicated the implications of the penultimate paragraph.

(b) There is little direct reference to this problem, but inferences can be made from the passage. These might be specific and show an apparently changing attitude (early resistance, later acceptance). Better still, one can infer from the passage that MacDonald's main purpose was to stay in power, and thus he would welcome a National Government if it enabled him to do so.

5. You may refer to the possibly loaded nature of the judgement in 4 (a) to undermine confidence. However, against this you must weigh the very detailed nature of the narrative; the even-handed way in which the priorities of the characters involved are dealt with; and the close referencing to sources.

6. The important thing here is to look at the nature of the evidence, which is opinion and hearsay—that MacDonald favoured the idea, and had re-aligned his own political thinking.

7. Even without knowing the standpoint of Snowden, it is clear that he is condemnatory. This can be seen in phrases such as 'too hurriedly' and 'highly agreeable' as well as the tenor of the whole passage.

8. It could be considered as a reliable indication of what colleagues of MacDonald thought, but not necessarily of what MacDonald thought.

9. You may wish to question some of the factual detail in A, but a better line of questioning concerns how Mowat used Snowden, which he has quoted in his sources.

10. Yes, but you should explain how.

11. There are clear differences here concerning MacDonald's intentions and reasons for changing his mind—you should explain these carefully.

12. An occasion for considering the standpoint and purpose of the writer. Davidson's party-political position may make him a more objective source than those more closely involved, and he appears to have been in a good position to know what was going on. As for MacDonald's diary . . . a good deal can be said. Remember not to confuse reliability with value.

13. 'mistaken mythology' is the key here. As for the reliability of the source, both the fact that it is recent and the broad view which it takes are encouraging.

14. Now its your turn to make some judgements.

C. CHECKLIST

1. Be aware of the distinction between primary evidence and secondary evidence, and the general characteristics of each.

2. Approach documents critically to establish the quality of information there. Understand them clearly by rewording or making précis.

3. Be aware of the context in which the document is set.

4. Be aware of external clues—citations, purpose of the writer. What do they indicate about the probable reliability of the document?

5. Is the document factually correct and full? Is it in agreement with other documents?

6. Can the interpretations be substantiated from the available evidence?

7. Is there any internal evidence which increases or decreases our confidence in the writer?

8. Of what value is the evidence for our particular purposes?

"Try to find as much primary evidence as possible."

REVISION

CHAPTER 6

About this Chapter

Revision should be an active and critical process. It should be carried out continuously and in parallel with other Advanced level work as part of a planned programme. Revision is a personal activity but the suggestions in this chapter try to make it a more effective, efficient and conscious process which will produce understanding. Memory should be a part of, and dependent on, understanding. Revision is an umbrella term for the processes of revising, review and recall.

A. UNDERSTANDING REVISION

Revision itself is an umbrella term, subject to a variety of usage, even abuse.

THE PROCESS OF REVISION: TERMS AND STAGES

Revision	The whole process of revising, review and recall.
1. Revising	The alteration, editing, questioning, reworking and addition of notes.
2. Reviewing	The refreshing of memory or re-reading for recall.
3. Recall	The remembering or calling into mind of information.

Far from reading this chapter at the end of a course or just before an examination, you need to consider Revision as soon as you start any piece of work. Memory is only partly your aim. You need also to understand the material you are studying.

> Revision should aim to create in your mind a permanent store of information which can be used efficiently.

Your ultimate aim in the examination is to have sufficient detail and range of information from which to select a full answer to the questions. As well as breadth and depth you will need familiarity and flexibility of knowledge, bred from understanding, to satisfy an individual question. Thus you can tackle any topic or problem which the examiner may place before you.

Unfortunately, because of their revision, many candidates will have only a limited view of each topic. Their revision methods hinder rather than help by triggering facts in an order and volume which may have little bearing on the question set. The question which does not line up perfectly with that limited view will either be impossible to answer or badly answered.

TWO PRINCIPLES SHOULD GUIDE YOUR REVISION

1. Revision is a process that begins almost as soon as you encounter new information and is continuous with all work.

2. Revision is an active and critical process.

STAGE 1: REVISE

Revision begins with revising your notes. Your ability to make notes will improve with time, but no set of notes will be perfect first time round. By revising your notes you should make good omissions, inaccuracies and weaknesses. In revising you are being critical of your notes and actively reworking them into a better form.

STAGE 2: REVIEW

After revising, review your notes. At this stage you are *rereading* your notes critically and contributing to your understanding. You may incorporate reviewing with active tasks of recall at a later stage (see p.136).

STAGE 3: RECALL

Recall is an activity which contributes to understanding and memory. You will notice the emphasis on activity or doing something. Passively staring at a page of notes prior to an examination and expecting the information to stick in your mind is not the best or most efficient way of learning. Regular or periodic activity is the best way to reinforce memory. For this reason regular reviews or rereadings are vital.

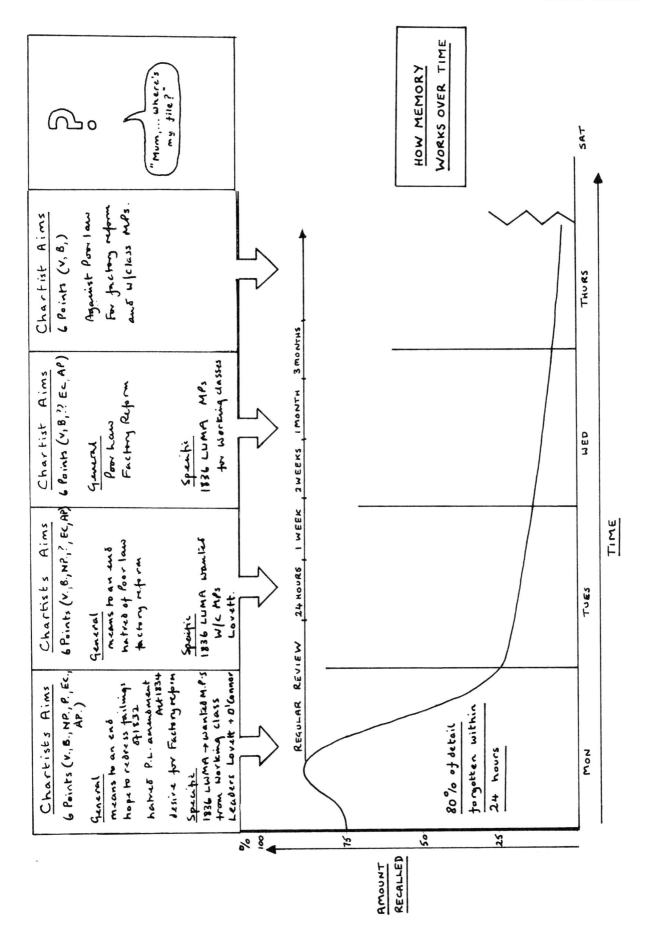

HOW WILL REVIEWING WORK HELP UNDERSTANDING AND MEMORY?

1. Consider the nursery rhymes you learned in infancy. You can remember them because they were often repeated and thus acquired a place in your long-term memory. The more frequently something is repeated, the more likely it is that you will remember it. Regular reviews will place information in your long-term memory 'painlessly'! They remove the need for memory 'cramming'.

2. It is wise to look at your notes while your understanding is fresh. Your notes are the essence of the information, a skeleton without the muscles to make it work. If you do not look at your notes within 24 hours of making them, much of the meaning of those notes will be lost.

3. Memory works by association and connection. Your ability to understand new information relies upon your ability to fit it into a pattern of existing knowledge. Rivalry in the Balkans makes more sense if you can recall the broader perspective of international relations. Lenin is better understood if you can appreciate the fundamentals of Marxism. Reviewing notes establishes these patterns of knowledge and makes understanding easier. Memory has been likened to a snowball: the more it rolls, the bigger it becomes, and eventually it will roll under its own momentum.

Without regular reviews you are depriving yourself of information, and therefore inhibiting further learning.

WHEN TO REVISE AND REVIEW NOTES

Try to revise notes the same day they are produced. A few hours after making notes is ideal. Reviews should then occur at regular intervals.

Time notes made	Purpose of revising/review	Possible length of time taken
1 day	Revising: Correct omissions, errors, misunderstandings	20-30 minutes
1 week	Review: Read for understanding	20 minutes maximum
2 weeks	Review	10 minutes
1 month	Review (and recall)	10 minutes
3 months	(Review, recall and further understanding.) Connections to related areas	15 minutes
6 months	Review and recall	10 minutes

The periods between reviews should be spaced progressively. The pattern in the table above is one possibility.

Reviewing will keep more information in your mind for longer and, when practised over time, will fix it there.

B. REVISING YOUR WORK: AN EXAMPLE

Consider the notes that follow and how a revised version has been produced.

Hitler Takes Power

In '32 elections - mixed success - at best,
Jan, 39.6% but by November NSDAP lost 2m votes

Hitler wouldn't form a coalition - and
couldn't get overall majority

Failure of Muller/Bruning/Pappen/Schlicher
came to Hitler's aid. Pappen proposed Hitler as
Chancellor, himself as V.C. He thought Hitler could
be controlled, and anyway Hitler didn't have a
majority. Hitler became Chancellor 30 Jan. 1933.

Then, during next campaign, Reichstag
Fire. Communists were blamed, Hitler given
emergency power, comms banned. In election
Hitler gained 43%. With other r.w. parties.
This gave him the majority of seats in the
Reichstag - To press the enabling act he needed
a 2/3 majority Using emergency power he backed
parliament with his own supporters and intimidated
other groups. - He gained a 2/3 majority and the
Enabling Act went through. This gave him total
power and made it possible

- To ban other parties
- To take control of the states' governments
- To make NSDAP the only legal party
- To ban Trade Unions and any other
  organisation which threatened his power

The campaign against other parties:
The main opposition came from the
Social Democrats, who had fought against
the enabling act despite intimidation from

[margin notes:]

Check these and later election results Why this loss of votes? See A.

* See notes on Weimar failure, above P Pappen? Ah! von Pappen Who is he? See B

★) Did they do it? See

Don't understand this. What is diff. between emergency power and Enabling Act?

Key Points - See

Essay Hitler p.

These notes, taken in class, are quite sound, and the student has sensibly left a broad margin for further comment and only written on one side of the paper. A thoughtful reading of them has thrown up a number of difficulties, minor errors, and gaps which need to be attended to while they are fresh.

FURTHER WORK TO BE DONE

Commentary

1. Elections of 1932. This needs expansion and explanation. No doubt the teacher gave it—it was not transmitted to the notes. See supplement A.

2. Papen. Since writing these notes, the correct spelling of Von Papen has been observed. Most spelling mistakes of this kind originate with words heard in lessons, but not seen. Examiners may well assume that this indicates a lack of reading! Here though, the correction has been made, and an explanation of the importance of Von Papen added in supplement B.

3. Reichstag fire. Obviously the teacher's remarks triggered some interest in the background to this. See supplement C.

4. There is confusion here between emergency powers and the Enabling Act. This difference must be clarified and the background to each explained.

5. At the end of the section it is a good moment to consider the demands of some 'A' level questions. See p.133 to show how this can in turn generate new activity.

6. These notes may be used for a précis or abstract. It is no coincidence that many commercial publishers have realised this need and sought to provide revision books or cards which mainly provide checklists or facts. What such cards offer is short-term hope of salvation, or at best confirmation that a student knows his stuff. What they do not allow for is a process of comprehending, sifting and streamlining notes, which is itself a vital learning process, and best done for yourself.

MAKING GOOD YOUR NOTES

Consider the results of revising and how it improved the original.

Supplements

A. Election Results. Source - A. Bullock, Hitler

Sept. 1930	18.3 % of votes cast
March 1932	30 %
April 1932	36.7 %
July 1932	37.3 %
Nov. 1932	33.1 %
March 1933	43.9 %

B. Franz Von Papen. Catholic, right wing, noble, powerful, industrialist, ex cavalry officer. Wanted German Empire. He became Chancellor in May 1932, but was unable to govern effectively without a majority. Being ambitious and unscrupulous, he believed he could rule through Hitler. This was his major blunder.

C. Emergency powers were allowed for within the Constitution. The "Decree for the protection of the People and the State" was aimed at the communists, giving Hitler full power and allowing him to increase penalties. Even so, any laws had to be ratified, so Hitler was not yet in a position of total power. The Enabling Law was a law to change the constitution thus a 2/3 majority needed. And Hitler would not be answerable to anyone for four years.

1) "To redress the alleged wrongs of the treaty of Versailles was only the first and least sinister of Hitlers ambitions in Foreign Policy." To what extent do you agree.

2) To what extent did Hitler gain power by constitutional means? (class essay)

3) Why and how, after becoming chancellor, was Hitler able to build a totalitarian state in Germany and uphold it during the rest of the 1930's?

4) What were the characteristics of German fascism. (class essay)

5) How do you explain the rise of Hitler to 1933?

HINTS

1. If you do not find the answers to problems or weaknesses revealed by revising, go to your teacher for help or advice on sources.

2. Supplementary notes should be inserted on the blank page facing the notes you are revising.

3. It is bad practice to generate many independent sets of notes relating to the same topic, as this can only make revision more laborious and confusing.

4. You should be able to find the time for revising notes very soon after they have been produced.

5. At first you should revise, review and recall alone! Cooperation with friends in revision may be supportive or productive but only at a later stage. It will not be useful in any way unless the information is first in your head to be tested or discussed.

6. To review regularly and make it a part of your normal work requires organisation and planning. Thus you should schedule work.

C. SCHEDULING YOUR WORK

1. THE AIM OF SCHEDULING

The overview and organisation of your work is vital. It should have, as its main aim, the efficient use of your time—which is a precious commodity.

2. STARTING A SCHEDULE

When you start a course you will not know the demands or nature of the work. So initially schedule work for one or two days. Work to this and see how you manage. Make any changes necessary as your understanding of the subject increases or weaknesses become evident. Then extend the schedule to other days and eventually a week. At the end of the first term, assess the effectiveness and efficiency of your system and plan for the next term.

3. FAULTS WITH SCHEDULES

The common faults with schedules of work are:

(a) starting with good intentions and then abandoning them. This will usually be because of lack of purpose or a fault in the schedule.

(b) being over-ambitious in setting tasks. This again leads to abandonment of the programme whereas changes to it would make it workable.

4. MAKING THE SYSTEM WORK

If you make a schedule or programme of work—stick to it. You will need determination, but give it time to work and make changes when you can see its weaknesses properly.

5. CYCLES OF WORK

AN EXAMPLE OF A REVISION CYCLE FOR A TWO A LEVEL STUDENT:

	Week 1	Week 2	Week 3
Monday	History E 30m	English 30m	History E 30m
Tuesday	English 20m	History PS 30m	English
Wednesday			
Thursday	History E 25m	English	History E 20m
Friday	English	History PS 15m	English
Saturday		English	(History/English) A optional 30m
Sunday	History/ A English (optional) 30m	History M 10m	

M Morning, A Afternoon, E Evening, PS Private Study

6. USING ALL AVAILABLE TIME

Make sure you use all available time efficiently, that is space set aside during the day for personal or private study. You can choose to review, make good, or revise notes during the day and liberate time in the evening for other pursuits or work.

7. THE PROBLEM OF INDEPENDENT STUDY

You will soon realise that work at Advanced level is demanding. You also have great freedom in organising your time. Self-discipline is needed to achieve your best. At one and the same time be realistic about what you can do but push yourself to do more!

8. TIMING

The amount of time you spend on the individual parts of your revision will vary. Working with small packets of time (15–20 minutes) will be most efficient. Short breaks of about 5 minutes are very important in keeping up your concentration and quality of work. But you need discipline to stick to a short break just as much as to stick to a schedule. Do not distract yourself in those 5 minute breaks, literally 'rest' your eyes, hands and brain, make a cup of coffee, stroke the cat or tidy up.

9. Similar schedules may be drawn up for holidays. Remember a rest from academic work is needed, so only schedule at most half the available time of a holiday period. You can complement your enjoyment of a break with the knowledge that you are consolidating your work and preparing for the next term.

An alternative way of scheduling and keeping track of work is on a topic by topic basis. Such a record may be kept at the beginning of a set of notes.

Hitler – Rise		Mussolini		Fascist Foreign Policy	
1, Revised	11 Nov	1, Revised	17 Nov	1, Revised	12 Nov
	12 Nov	2, Made good	18 Nov		14 Nov
	14 Nov	3, Reviewed	25 Nov		17 Nov
			2 Dec	2, Made good	19 Nov
2, Made good	16 Nov		16 Dec	3, Reviewed	26 Nov
			14 Jan		3 Dec
3, Reviewed	23 Nov				10 Dec
	30 Nov				17 Dec
	14 Dec				
	11 Jan				

In a schedule you can see at a glance what revision you have done for each topic and project forward to what is still needed.

D. REVIEW AND RECALL

So far we have considered:

(a) revising notes continuously.

(b) planning regular reviews of work done.

This will make revision more purposeful and in the long term less laborious.

Reviewing work will greatly increase recall but weaknesses or gaps may exist. Some work can be done to aid recall, consolidate and extend understanding. All such work must actively involve you in reworking the material. Even throwing away rough compilations or analyses based on your notes will do no harm. The important thing is that you have been thinking about the information; it is still in your main notes. Furthermore you must be willing to experiment with techniques. There are many methods of promoting understanding and memory, not all will suit you or the subject matter. Experiment until you find a system which suits you.

The Précis, Abstract or Digest

An activity which clarifies and gives a priority to information is useful. You may choose to produce a parallel card system as a digest of significant points, interpretations or key ideas. You will be using the skills of notemaking and document work together. Try to make such a system do more than briefly reproduce your notes. Ask questions about linking themes, cross reference with other periods or countries. You will find some possible 'new' questions in textbooks and essay titles.

Rapid Review and Recall

In later reviews you may try this method of rapid review and recall, rather than thoughtful and critical re-reading. Carefully read a page of your file and turn the page. On rough paper, jot down briefly all that you can remember.

Look back and see what you missed. Without dwelling on the parts you could not recall, tackle the next page. Work through a topic in this manner. When you repeat the process the next day your stock of knowledge of that topic should have risen. Eventually, the amount forgotten should dwindle to nothing.

Cluster Revision: An example of an advanced system.

In this example a student has tried to grapple with historical understanding in a direct way by using clusters of information and formulating new questions for them. A cluster is centred on a question and a number of points which go to support it. It is not suggested that you copy this system but there are important lessons to be learned from it and you might then try to solve the basic problem for yourself.

1. The student has decided on a topic, key points and supporting evidence.

2. The key points are decided by asking a question e.g. Topic: Adolf Hitler. Question: How do you explain his rise to power?

3. Six key points are thought of or formed in the student's notes in much the same way as in question analysis. They might represent paragraphs in the final essay.

4. The question is placed on the horizontal axis and the key points on the vertical axis of the chart or matrix.

5. Another question is posed, e.g. What were the characteristics of German Fascism?

6. Between five and seven points may be produced and so the chart is built up.

7. In the intersecting boxes comments are added to explain the significance or relationship of key points to the question.

Key Points	1. 'First and least sinister?	2. Power by constitutional means?	3. Totn. State	4. Characteristics of Fascism	5. Rise of Hitler
Outcome of 1914-18 war	✓				
Versailles	✓ ① Alleged wrongs				preconditions inc. *
Reparations	in part.				
Occupation of Ruhr	✓				
Economy		appeal of Nazism			
Hitler - background	③ Sinister ambition			unique elements	Hitler & appeal
– philosophy	✓ Lebensraum				
– Mein kampf	✓ ↓				
Early NSDAP				✓ origins	
Munich Putsch					vote winning
Electoral tactics		✓		✓	
SA/SS		*			* and outcomes
Weimar failures					
1932 Elections		✓) "genuine" vote winning	✓ Intro	*	political manouvring
Chancellor			means to dictator-ship		
Reichstag Fire		with * dubious nature of these			
Emergency powers					
Enabling Act					
Single part				✓ the system	
State govt		Outcomes - constitutional?	holding on to		
End of unions					
Long knives					
Presidency				*Single leader	
Ec. policy				✓ policy	
Educn. and prop			maintain	Fascist State	
Anti-semitism					
Totaln. State				✓ policy	
Lebensraum	✓ ② Relate to Versailles				
Rearmament	✓				
Rhineland					
Anschluss	✓ ④ Beyond Versailles				
Czech.a	✓				
Poland	✓ (but, n.b, Danzig]				

THE VALUE OF SUCH A SYSTEM

1. Cluster revision involves all three revision activities—revising, reviewing, and recall. It changes the natural sequence of information i.e. chronology or narrative, which may strongly influence what you write in the examination. Cluster revision imposes a new, flexible structure on information.

2. Information needs to be assessed for its worth or significance. You must be able to separate minor from major points. Cluster revision encourages the process of selection and the ability to understand relative importance. This is a vital skill when answering examination questions.

3. There is no simple way of identifying main or key points. Cluster revision is useful because it gives practice in using the resources at your disposal, e.g. teacher notes, essay questions, text books etc.

4. You must be willing to experiment and formulate questions in revision. This system may seem mechanical or laborious. Certainly it requires time and effort, but it is original, critical and active.

5. The aim of revision should be to produce better understanding. The cluster system shows one way this may be achieved and it lends itself to the writing of essays.

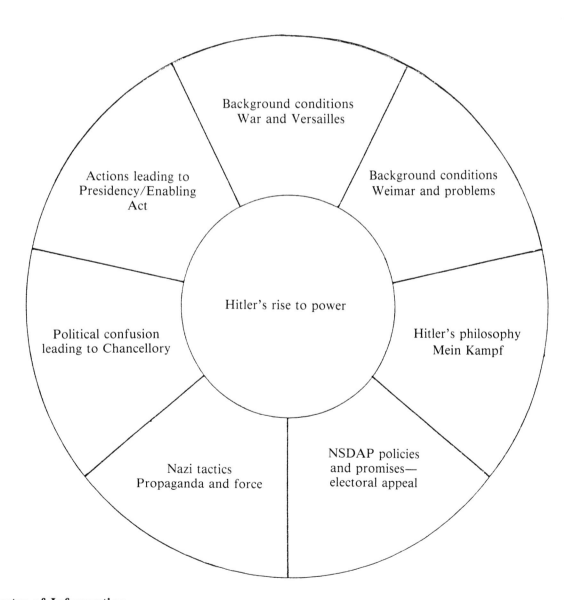

A Cluster of Information

E. REMEMBERING INFORMATION

You may choose to adopt one or all of the ideas recommended in this chapter. Whether you use them or not, you should have some system which processes and produces material in such a way that *you* control the information and *not* the other way round.

Some methods of gaining familiarity with notes have already been mentioned, and these will contribute greatly to permanent recall. Furthermore, concentration under examination conditions may encourage you to draw from deep in the memory.

However, most people will rightly want to add a detailed knowledge of specific information—for example, the detail of digests, abstracts or other processed information. There are various possible ways of doing this. Again the important thing is to approach the task purposefully and with a method or system.

Memory Methods: An example

Consider the notes on Hitler's rise to power. Essay answers to this question are notorious for their adherence to narrative. The revision of the chronology of Hitler's rise is likely to continue the pattern. However, revision of a group cluster of significant points can be far more productive.

1. TITLING

Give them a title, reduce, clarify, summarise the information into a memorable heading:

'The Enabling Act'

2. ASSOCIATION

Find a suitable way of remembering.

(a) *By number*
There are seven points here. Remember the number in association with the title. The number is your checklist.

(b) *By letters*
Mnemonics—letter form. From this list you can identify key words to form a series such as VW Hatch.

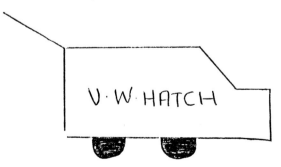

Hitler's Rise

(1) **V**ersailles settlement
(2) **W**eimar weaknesses
(3) **H**itlers background + philosophy
(4) **A**ppeal of Hitlers programme
(5) **T**actics of Nazis
(6) **C**hancellory
(7) **H**itler in power as dictator

V·W·HATCH

However, this method can become more trouble than it is worth, and is best with straightforward series.

(c) *By mental picture*
In your mind create an image. Hitler, standing on a platform labelled 'Versailles War Guilt' and 'Weimar Weakness', a gun in his right hand labelled 'S.A.', a sheaf of documents in his left hand labelled 'promises'. Fawning at his side are politicians hoping to use him to increase their own influence. Above him is the swastika, the image of Nazi propaganda. Under his right boot lies a person, the Star of David clearly displayed, and another with a badge saying Social Democrat. Behind him burns the Reichstag, and within the flames the words Enabling Act can be seen.

3. DIAGRAMS

Techniques for remembering and self-testing can be equally imaginative using diagrams. Consider the type of notes for 'brainstorming' for example, on p.57. Pattern notes are also useful not only for generating information, but also for making links across subject areas. Indeed, a complex pattern note could well be used to supplement or even replace the cluster chart.

F. USING ESSAYS FOR REVISION: THE DANGER

There are many good reasons why you should not regard essays as a helpful source of information for revision.

1. Essays are bound to have failings as answers to a question set—especially those essays written early in the course. The structure, argument and information content will have omissions and errors which should not be built into a revision programme.

2. The purpose of writing essays is the exercise of historical skills. Thus the information content is of secondary importance.

Some 'essays' may have been completed which contain original information. These may be more properly termed 'research papers'. Their original or new information should have been transferred and incorporated into your notes.

3. The essay is the answer to one question. Revision of an already flawed essay in hope that the same question, or a close variation, will appear on the paper, is madness.

CAN ANYTHING BE SALVAGED FROM ESSAYS?

There should be no information in essays which is not in your notes, and they will be far more helpful for revision. Possibly there will be some paragraphs in the essay which can be used individually as key points, but this will depend on the quality of the essay. Finally, the most useful part of the essay will be the teacher's comments. You should have borne these in mind throughout the course, and perhaps built a self-criticism from them. Reminding yourself of where you went wrong could well be a useful part of a revision process, and could promote remedial action.

G. EXAMINATION PRACTICE AND REVISION

The importance of asking questions of your notes cannot be over-emphasised. Your teacher can help you by providing these questions either for paragraph answers or as essay titles. Revision may be combined with examination practice by writing 'timed' essays and essay plans of ten to fifteen minutes each. You will need to be able to think and write quickly in the examination. However, the questions you answer must be sufficiently different from the ones you may have tackled during the course. The main purpose of the timed essay is not to test your memory but your ability to think, adjust and select from your knowledge to meet a new challenge or understand a different perspective on a problem, within a given time. The questions or timed essays you write should aim to increase the breadth and depth of your understanding in preparation for the examination.

H. CHECKLIST

1. All revision should be active, critical and part of a continuous programme.

2. Revision begins with a revising of your notes.

3. Revise to make your notes more complete—correct errors, fill gaps, clarify and explain difficult points.

4. Regularity and repetition of review is important.

5. The examination requires breadth and depth of knowledge.

6. The questions require familiarity and flexibility with the information.

7. A digest of information, if constructed in a different way from your main notes and at the end of a period of regular review, can be very useful.

8. Rapid review and recall as a part of a programme of revision will help reduce the volume of material to be learned.

9. A system like the cluster revision system has advantages because:
   (a) it actively involves you with the information.
   (b) it creates flexibility and mental agility with the material.

10. Remember information by giving sub-headings, titles, by association and with diagrams.

11. Using old essays for revision is likely to reproduce old errors and cause a rigidity of mind which will prevent you answering properly the question set.

12. You can revise best by yourself. There are no shortcuts to revision.

THE EXAMINATION

About this Chapter

This chapter will not attempt to distil the complete contents of the whole book. It will provide some guidance on the final approach to the examination, the importance of the first thoughtful minutes of confrontation with the paper, and some specific points about essay writing which will help demonstrate your ability to the examiner.

NOTE

Do not turn straight to this chapter in order to find an easy route to examination success! In the same way that the examination is the logical culmination of a two year History course, this chapter is only a conclusion to a book which has been concerned with the skills of the advanced study of History. It would also be wrong, having completed a History course, to feel that the examination is separate from the work of two years. The examination is not a last great hurdle intended to trip the candidate. It is meant to be the opportunity for the student to express the skills, understanding and knowledge acquired over those two years. Neither is the examination unpredictable. To a large extent the final result will be consistent with your level of achievement over those two years. Don't worry, the examination is your opportunity to confirm the achievement of two years' work.

A. BEFORE THE EXAMINATION

1. Your revision timetable, which should have been carefully planned over the past weeks and months, should finally be keyed into the examination calendar in accordance with the distribution of your papers.

2. It is best if you do not discuss revision, anticipated topics, mnemonics or other devices outside the examination room. It is often true that empty vessels make most noise—but they may also undermine your confidence at a vital moment.

3. Check your pen, and keep a spare. Amazingly, each year, a great deal of time is wasted on faulty, leaking pens, or on borrowing replacements.

B. THE RUBRIC

Do not take the instructions on the front of the examination paper (the rubric) for granted. You should have studied the rubric well in advance of the examination. Make sure that you understand it. Ask your teacher if you don't. Some are very straightforward—'Answer four essays', for example. Others do set important limits on what you can do by placing questions in sections.

e.g:

'Answer four questions, including Question 1 and either Question 2 or Question 3 from Section (2) and two questions from Section (3).'

Get this wrong and the offending answer will be struck out with no reward. It happens to a disturbing number of people every year!

C. ADOPTING A STRATEGY FOR THE WHOLE PAPER

It is unwise to open the examination paper and think only of the first question.

> 'Another frequent weakness which handicaps many candidates is that of uneven performance.'
>
> (J.M.B. Examiners' Report:
> A level History, 1979, p.37)

In order to achieve a good result, a sound fourth question is just as important as a sound first question, and you must have the resources—historical knowledge and understanding, energy, and time—to do the last question justice. After all, in a paper of four essay questions, no candidate can afford to be marked out of 75 instead of 100 marks. This is what happens if you only have time to answer 3 questions. To put it another way, to pass you have to obtain the equivalent of 53% of the marks if you only do three questions (40/75)!!

Historical knowledge and understanding will be the product of two years work and adequate revision. Energy will vary from person to person, and should affect the way in which you select questions. If you have learned from the experience of trial examinations that you tend to start a paper slowly and warm up, tackle what you consider to

be the most straightforward question first. If you tend to start well, then fade away and lose energy and inspiration, tackle the most challenging question first and leave the more straightforward question until later.

If there is a single evidence question on your paper, do that first, but do not overrun. The reason for tackling this question first is that it tends to gain more marks than essays, and thus should not be denied time or energy by being placed at the end. Perhaps, too, this style of question should not be allowed to break up the flow of essays.

Timing is also of key importance. It is often the case that candidates allow themselves only a few minutes for the last question. This could be disastrous and might well mean a difference of two grades on the paper.

> 'It should not be necessary to remind candidates that time is precious and should not be frittered away unproductively. The consequence of doing so is frequently a hurried and fragmentary last answer or even two answers: a self inflicted wound that few candidates can afford.'
>
> (J.M.B. Examiners' Report:
> A level History, 1982, p.44)

The first task when faced with an examination paper is to *read it through, slowly and carefully*. Even if this advice is remembered in the panic and pressure of the examination room, many candidates will react too quickly to the first impressions created by the questions, almost unconsciously selecting and eliminating them. It is vital at this time to have the right mental attitude. Exercise *self control*, show calmness and deliberateness, read the questions very slowly for a *second time*. Don't prejudge on a quick initial reading. Ignore other people. Approach the questions in front of you objectively and coolly. After a second reading you should be familiar with the paper. Examine each question in turn, weighing it up in your mind. Use the skills of question analysis. Identify the questions which appeal to or interest you. Select those you will answer and decide upon an order for proceeding with them. Begin your planning.

This may well take the first five or ten minutes of the examination. The first two questions should take no more than forty-five minutes each, leaving forty each for the others. If the first three essays exceed this guideline by only five minutes each, it will leave only twenty minutes for the last essay, which still carries a quarter of the marks.

Remember that it is the form or line of argument of your essay which will determine the mark range of your answer, and that the detail which you provide in support will only add or detract a little from this. It is therefore essential that each essay has a form—but the sort of supplementary detail which so often causes essays to overrun can easily be cut.

Alternatively, you should never have time to spare at the finish. If you do, it will be beneficial to read back to check for errors, omissions and paragraph links. This is a luxury, and of course it is best to plan and concentrate well enough along the way to render re-reading unnecessary.

Remember, too, it is what you write that counts.

—Do not write out the question.
—Do not use liquid paper—one line through an error, or a whole paragraph, will do.
—Do not cross out material to insert something which you have forgotten. Use an asterisk and indicate to the examiner where a subsequent sentence or paragraph will be inserted.
—Do not waste time with elaborate handwriting, looped full stops—simply write as fast as your hand and mind co-ordination allows, yet keeping your writing legible.

Examiners are interested in what you have to say, and rarely is a legible essay penalised for scrappy writing. Yet elegant copperplate handwriting, if it is not expressing worthwhile historical ideas, will gain nothing. Bearing in mind earlier advice, you should first identify which questions you intend to answer. To do this you have to think carefully, and may need to make a preliminary plan for more than four essays to decide which suit you best.

Before starting your first essay you may wish either:

    (a) to plan all your answers in detail.
or (b) to plan, then write each in turn.
or (c) to adopt a strategy of planning two, then returning to write the first. While the second plan is being constructed, your

ideas for the first plan will have had time to settle, and you can return to it afresh. On completing your first essay, plan three, then return to reconsider the plan for two, then write it.

In your trial examination, and as part of your revision programme, experiment with what suits you best.

D.   SELECTING YOUR QUESTIONS CAREFULLY

The choice of questions will be crucial in determining your level of achievement, and so requires thought and time.

1. Resist the temptation to begin writing too soon. Consider each question carefully.

2. Do not make the mistake of searching the paper for familiar topics. Use the skills of question analysis to decide whether or not a particular question is the right one for you to tackle.

3. What is the question about?
    (a) Is the subject matter what it seems? By Bolshevik Revolution does the examiner mean both revolutions of 1917 or only October?
    (b) Is there any chronological definition? A question on British foreign policy 1902–7 may well defy the candidate who has a more general knowledge of international relations before 1914.
    (c) Is a familiar topic disguised under another label? 1833–41 should be instantly identifiable as a significant Whig ministry, and other important ministries of the nineteenth century may also be classified by date rather than name. Alternatively a label may be used, and no dates supplied.

4. What is the question asking about these topics?
    (a) The commands: 'To what extent', 'Assess the success/failure', 'How far', 'Discuss', are crucial—as important, if not more so, than the subject itself, because they should determine the direction of the essay and the material to be selected. Practice in essay writing, and the use of a flexible cluster revision system will enable students to . . .

'distinguish and differentiate between the specific requirements of different kinds of questions and to be more able to shape their material to the dictates of the questions. In the answers to a number of questions this year it was evident that candidates had the requisite information but failed to do justice to their factual knowledge by producing responses that were too close in form to a set of classroom notes or even to a prepared essay.'

(J.M.B. Examiners' Report:
A level History. 1983, p.31)

'The more successful candidates are those who perceptively take advantage of . . . the wording of questions, deciding where the emphasis lies and then writing an answer directed to that emphasis.'

(J.M.B. Examiners' Report:
A level History, 1983, p.36)

(b) Has the question more than one part? If so, do not forget to give each part its due, weighting your answer according to your interpretation of the question.

'Most disturbing is . . . a failure to answer all parts of a set question; the ignoring of opening and closing dates.'

(J.M.B. Examiners' Report:
A level History, 1979, p.37)

(c) Don't be frightened of *quotations*. Often the quotation can be seen as an essay plan in microcosm.

'Candidates should be encouraged to look closely at such questions for often the phrasing not only points clearly to what is required but also provides a sound indication of a structured approach for an answer.'

(J.M.B. Examiners' Report:
A level History, 1979, p.37)

E. THE ESSAY PLAN

You would perhaps be surprised to read in one examiner's report that some of the best answers are of quite moderate length, but they impress through their precision and economy of effort. It cannot be over-emphasised that there is no virtue in sheer volume. Quantity of material will earn far less reward than clarity of thought, and that comes from taking a few minutes to think out the way in which an essay will develop.

Plans can be misused

It is astonishing, but true, that each year some candidates write whole essays in pencil, make minor corrections, then rewrite them in ink. This is fortunately rare, but other examples of poor use of plans are frequently seen. Take these examples:

"Chartism was a knife and fork question." To what extent does the history of the Chartist movement bear out this judgement?

Plan

- Universal Sufferage
- Annual Parliament
- Equal electricald. sts.
- payment of MPs
- secret ballot
- ?

London WMA 1836
Lovett
moral/Physical
petitions
plug plots/Newport
Failed year of
rev. 1848

Consider the factors influencing Anglo - German relations, 1904-14

Plan

Morocco   1905
Dreadnought 1906 .
Balkan Crisis
Agadir   1911
Haldane   1912
Sarajevo / Schlieffen.

This is, in fact, not so much a plan as a brief reminder of what the candidate considers to be key points. The fact that this student knows them makes their appearance here irrelevant—unless, of course, he fears that they are likely to be forgotten in the next few minutes. Worse than being a waste of time, they might dictate the course of the essay, which would bring disaster. This plan does nothing constructive and could impose a narrative structure and a lack of direction.

Now consider this plan, for the same question:

> "Chartism was a Knife and fork question". To what extent does the history of the Chartist movement bear out this judgement?
>
> Knife + fork = economic   V   Chartism as pol movement
>
> support this view   this to an extent too
>
> land mechanism   Failure of GNCTU
>
> anti-poor law   good yrs. of Chm = harvest failure   6 points   Outwardly   leadership
>
> origin in 1832   methods

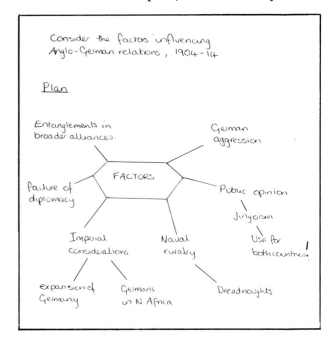

> Consider the factors influencing Anglo-German relations, 1904-14
>
> Plan
>
> Entanglements in broader alliances   German aggression
>
> failure of diplomacy   FACTORS   Public opinion
>
> Imperial considerations   Naval rivalry   Jingoism
>
> expansion of Germany   Germans in N Africa   Dreadnoughts   Use for both countries.

ADVANTAGES OF THIS TYPE OF PLAN

1. It provides a structure for the essay. By the time the plan is complete, the student can visualise the appearance of the whole essay. Key points represent paragraphs. Details can be added where helpful, but are not allowed to overwhelm the structure. If, while writing the essay, other important points come to mind, they can quickly be added to the plan and used in the appropriate place. Having identified the key points, they have also been numbered to show the order in which they will be considered.

2. It is a memory aid. During the construction of a plan the student is likely to think of a number of main points and details in swift succession. The plan can enable the student who is worried about 'drying up' to get these ideas on paper quickly.

3. The plan is not cramped at the top of a page. It should be written on loose paper (which can be tied to the answer booklet at the end of the examination). This will allow ample space, and the plan can be consulted at any time without shuffling back to the beginning of the essay.

4. Of course, pattern notes do not work for everyone. A linear plan can do just as well, but leave space to develop ideas further, and having established key points, use numbering so that the plan still has flexibility.

5. By the time that you have thought out a plan, you will be better prepared to write your introduction as a keynote to what is to follow.

F. INTRODUCTIONS

Having heeded the advice in Essay Writing you may well have developed a formula for writing introductions for class essays. Such a formula can and should be used in examinations, but should be crisp. Thus, if you are not the type of candidate with the ability to write at great length, or if you are short of time, use a three sentence formula rather than one of six sentences. The examiner will be impressed or depressed by the first words of any answer. Too often the introduction serves only as a rephrasing of the question.

Consider these two examples:

"Chartism was a knife and fork question"
To what extent does the history of the Chartist movement bear out this judgement?

The Chartist movement began by demanding political rights for the working classes. They saw the vote, secret ballot and better representation as the only way to break the hold of the wealthy classes on government. The movement began in 1838 with the formation of the "London Working Men's association" by William Lovett.

Consider the factors which influenced Anglo-German relations between 1904 and 1914.

The years 1900-14 saw a steady deteriotation of Anglo-German relations. Crisis followed crisis, and the assassination of Archduke Franz-Ferdinand was only the spark and by no means the cause of a war which could have broken out any time in the preceding years.

Neither of these will impress. They are thoughtless and make no impact whatsoever on the question. Much more impressive would be:

"Chartism was a knife and fork question"
To what extent does the History of the
Chartist movement bear out this judgement?

Chartism was a working class movement
which dominated the decade to 1848.
Overtly the movement was a political one:
yet massive research into Chartism has
shown it to have been borne out of working
class distress — a knife and fork question.
This examination will focus on the latter,
then attempt to reconcile it's economic
origins with it's political demands.

Consider the factors which influenced Anglo-German
relations between 1904 and 1914

The first fifteen years of the twentieth century saw
the might of Britain and her Empire being challenged by
the young ambitious Germany. Relations between the two
were influenced by the conflicting aims and standpoints
of each, and by the complex shifting of international
diplomacy around them. This analysis will deal with the
factors which accelerated the deterioration of relationships
and the eventual outbreak of war between them.

G. WRITING THE ESSAY

Your response to the question in the examination is the embodiment of all the skills discussed in the earlier chapters of this book. It will depend on the range and depth of your reading, your ability in making notes, your perception in question analysis, and your ability in writing essays.

Only a few pieces of specific guidance can be added:

1. Bring your answer down to the scale of the examination. Whereas in a class essay you may have argued a point and given three detailed examples, now there will only be time for one, with passing reference to the others.

2. By the time of the examination some of the information you use will be very familiar—for example ideas about topics covered early in the course may have been trotted out twice in internal examinations. Now, however, you must assume that they are fresh ideas as far as your examiner is concerned. Certainly the argument or the way you use the information will have to be apt and original.

3. Be careful with paragraphing. Paragraphs should follow a logical plan, and each successive paragraph should add a different theme to the essay. In each case, link the paragraph to what has gone before and to the essay title, explain the new theme, and give an example or examples to support it.

4. These links are vital. They are the best way to make your writing explicit and relevant. They are also a good way of keeping your answer firmly in line with the question. Indeed at intervals you should glance back to the question, and make sure that you have not strayed.

H. CONCLUSIONS

By the time that you begin to write your conclusion the merit of your answer will already be taking shape in the examiner's mind. The conclusion will confirm what has already been learned from the essay, and will only bring a minor adjustment. Thus, keep it crisp. The conclusion should not introduce any new material. It is an opportunity to confront the title, and show how your answer differs from or qualifies that question. The examiners complain that conclusions generally . . .

'follow one of three strategies: they present laboured repetition of an argument, already brief and easily recalled, and effecting no argument or improvement to the argument outlined; final paragraphs readily identified from their 'thus it can be seen' format, which at the end of a long undirected narration, attempt to attain some direction and relation to the terms of the question: or fumbling efforts to summarise which mar rather than enhance.'

(J.M.B. Examiners' Report: A level History, 1980, p.20)

Alternatively, a fine conclusion, rounding off an impressive piece of work which displays all the skills of the young historian will bring forth these much more encouraging comments:

'The best candidates continue to produce work which (if the boot were on the other foot) the examiners would have been proud to have offered.'

(J.M.B. Examiners' Report: A level History, 1982, p.51–2)

I. CHECKLIST

1. Be prepared.

2. Know what to expect.

3. When you open your paper:

   —Have a system in mind.

   —Apply the techniques of question analysis to all 'possibles'.

4. Plan each answer carefully on a loose sheet of paper.

5. In your introduction, paragraph links, themes and examples, tell the examiner exactly what the question demands. Bear the question in mind at all times!

6. Keep your eye on the clock.

'Be prepared!'

ACKNOWLEDGEMENTS

The authors are grateful to the Joint Matriculation Board and the London University Examination Board for permission to use quotations from their Examiners' Reports.

The authors and publishers wish to thank the following for permission to reprint copyright material:

R. J. Cootes and *Radio Times* Hulton Picture Library for the picture from *Britain Since 1700* (London, 1968) p. 191; Kenneth O. Morgan and Weidenfeld & Nicholson Ltd for the extract from *Lloyd George* (London, 1974) pp. 200, 201, 205; H. Hearder and Longman for the two extracts from *Europe in the Nineteenth Century* (London, 1966) pp. 181, 96; Asa Briggs and Longman for the extract from *The Age of Improvement, 1783–1867* (London, 1959) pp. 236–268; Michael Brock and Century Hutchinson for the extract from *The Great Reform Act* (London, 1973) pp. 250–253; R. Kedward and Macdonald for the extracts from *The Anarchists* (London, 1971); E. J. Evans and Longman for the extract from *The Forging of the Modern State, 1783–1870* (London, 1983) pp. 338–9; J. M. Roberts and Longman for the short extract from *Europe 1880–1945* (London, 1972); E. J. Feuchtwanger and Penguin Books for the short extracts from *Gladstone* (London, 1975) pp. 230, 280, © E. J. Feuchtwanger, 1975; Tony Buzan and BBC Publications for the extract from *Use Your Head* (London, 1974); A. J. P. Taylor and Oxford University Press for the short extract from *English History, 1914–45* (Oxford, 1965) p. 387; J. Plamenatz and Longman for the short extract from *Man and Society, Vol 2* (London, 1963) p. 94; A. E. Musson and Macmillan for the short extract from *British Trade Unions 1800–1875* (London, 1972) p. 40; Henry Pelling and Macmillan for the extracts from *Popular Politics and Society in Late Victorian Britain* (2nd ed. London, 1979); Anne Digby, P. Searby and Macmillan for the extract from *Children, School and Society in 19th Century England* (London, 1981) p. 49; F. S. L. Lyons and Weidenfeld (Publishers) Ltd for the extract from *Ireland since the Famine* (London, 1973) p. 556; J. Vincent and Constable for the extract from *The Formation of the British Liberal Party* (Harmondsworth, 1966) p. 261; E. H. Carr and Macmillan for the extract from *What is History* (Harmondsworth, 1964) p. 23; B. Porter and Longman for the extract from *The Lion's Share: A Short History of British Imperialism 1850–1983* (2nd ed. London, 1984) p. 339; R. Evans and Edward Arnold for the extract from *The Victorian Age* (London, 1950) p. 193; Charles Loch Mowat and Methuen for the extract from *Britain between the Wars* (London, 1955).

Every effort has been made to trace and acknowledge copyright holders. The publishers apologise for any infringement of copyright and would be glad to hear from any unacknowledged copyright holders.